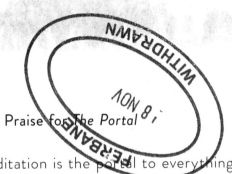

Praise for *The Portal*

'I believe meditation is the portal to everything
and in my experience with Tom, he's the
man to step you through this journey.
A new, better world awaits.'

LISA MESSENGER, FOUNDER AND EDITOR-IN-CHIEF,
COLLECTIVE HUB

'Perhaps the most important message
the world needs to hear.'

JACK DELOSA, ENTREPRENEUR, INVESTOR
AND CEO OF THE ENTOURAGE

'*The Portal* is a compelling and practical blueprint
to realise the potential of human civilisation.'

KAT DUNN, CEO OF GRAMEEN AUSTRALIA

'With a rare blend of unabashed optimism
and deep thoughtfulness, *The Portal* explores
the possibility of partnering technology with
human consciousness to envision a sane
and sustainable future for humanity.'

KAISA PUHAKKA, PHD

THE

PORTAL

THE

PORTAL

TOM CRONIN
AND JACQUI FIFER

murdoch books

Sydney | London

Published in 2019 by Murdoch Books, an imprint of Allen & Unwin

Murdoch Books Australia
83 Alexander Street, Crows Nest NSW 2065
Phone: +61 (0)2 8425 0100
murdochbooks.com.au
info@murdochbooks.com.au

Murdoch Books UK
Ormond House, 26–27 Boswell Street, London WC1N 3JZ
Phone: +44 (0) 20 8785 5995
murdochbooks.co.uk
info@murdochbooks.co.uk

A catalogue record for this
book is available from the
National Library of Australia

A catalogue record for this book is available from the British Library

ISBN 978 1 76052 409 8 Australia
ISBN 978 1 91163 205 4 UK

Cover and internal design by Madeleine Kane
Photography © Superhuman International Pty Ltd except where noted
Cover art by the Trace House

Printed and bound in Australia by Griffin Press

10 9 8 7 6 5 4 3 2 1

For you: the reader of these words.

Your challenges, your turmoil, your, and our,

highs and lows were the inspiration for this book.

May we all find that quiet meeting point,

amid the turbulence of life, where our unique

stories and differences come together

and things make sense.

CONTENTS

'It's a brilliant gift to be human.'

RABBI RONNIE CAHANA

INTRODUCTION

For thousands of years, the question has been asked:
How do you get through the turbulence of life?

We are hurtling towards a pivotal moment for humanity, a point in time when what we do next could determine the future of our species. Economic, environmental, technological and humanitarian experts suggest we are nearing an unrecoverable crisis point for life on our planet. It's a situation that historian and cognitive scientist Noam Chomsky describes as a perfect storm, one that could lead to a breakdown of civilisation as we know it unless something changes—fast.[1]

On a personal level, it seems that no matter where you travel or who you meet, people are feeling the intensity of modern life, and are struggling to find happiness and focus amid its relentless turbulence. Technology, the internet, the smartphone: they were all going to make our lives simpler, weren't they? We have made incredible technological advances, and we in the West have access to more abundance than ever before, but how are we actually feeling right now? Our minds and hearts are taking a battering and, for many people, it's hard to tell whether things are getting better—or worse.

So as the media and society push us to find solace in quick fixes and the eternal quest for 'more' (antidotes that many argue have contributed to us being in this mess), what if we could find a more sustainable way to feel the personal benefits of a life well lived? One that didn't result in crippling the planet that supports our very existence? Making the solution personal is what this book is about.

As a transformational coach and meditation teacher, Tom has seen people get caught up time and again in unsustainable patterns of behaviour that usually result from outdated ways of thinking about things. More often than not, it takes some life-changing event or crisis—essentially a fork in the road—for them to even realise this is happening. At this juncture, they either break down into more negative patterns and chaos (sadly, this sometimes means a person even takes their own life), or they break through into a more orderly and progressive way of living, upgrading their mind and its outdated 'programming'.

The Vedas, a large body of sacred texts written in India more than three thousand years ago, talked of a cataclysmic event or force so pervasive and powerful it would be capable of shaking up even the most persistent of situations. This event, referred to in Sanskrit as a *rashi*, was considered an instrument of evolution. When we face a rashi, we are essentially *forced* to change. We must either find a new way to move forwards, or we are thrown into such a destructive situation that deterioration occurs on a grand scale: people die, marriages end, companies collapse or countries are thrown into chaos and civil unrest. This book includes personal stories from people who have been through just those sorts of experiences.

Humans are a highly adaptable species, and yet we can be incredibly stubborn and resistant to change. In writing this book, we explore the question: Is society as a whole caught up in outdated patterns of behaviour that have led us to a global crisis—a collective fork in the road—that will see us break *down* or break *through*? And if so, is there anything we can do about it?

Tom's story

It was my own crisis—my rashi—and subsequent transformation that became a big inspiration for this book. In February 1996, I had a nervous breakdown. It was the culmination of years of negative thought patterns and excess of every kind: an addiction to success, money and the adrenaline highs of my life as a broker. It didn't occur to me to make a change, yet I felt trapped, mired in spiralling depression and panic, even questioning whether to continue with life. One morning, while getting ready for work, I collapsed on the floor. I thought I was having a heart attack. I thought, *This is it*—and I didn't really care. My severe symptoms eventually landed me in the clinic of a leading psychiatrist, who prescribed medication.

I started to feel less anxious on the drugs, but they also made me feel 'checked out' and numb. Even more numb than before. The sadness and loneliness lingered and, deep inside, I sensed this wasn't the way forwards. It was at that time that I first came across meditation and Eastern philosophy. From then on, everything in my life began to change.

Meditation was like a portal into another realm. Angst and debilitating fear were replaced with an inner peace that I had never felt before. Sleep returned. I could leave the house and be around people again. The rapid change stunned me.

For thousands of years, sages and spiritual masters have been experiencing enlightenment, bliss and unconditional love in caves, ashrams and monasteries all over the world. Now, here I was, smack bang in the middle of a city, and I was experiencing it too. I found out that the things I'd been looking for my entire life in nightclubs, drugs and money were inside me all along. At the time, no one else in my circle was meditating. Why weren't more people doing this? Wasn't this what we *all* wanted?

Through my studies of meditation and Eastern philosophy, I went on to learn more about the mind and why I had always looked outside of myself for happiness. I learned about the underlying factors that had led me into such dire straits that I absolutely *had* to make a drastic change, and about why getting what I deeply, deeply wanted had seemed so elusive. I learned about various spiritual traditions, including Buddhism and the Vedic philosophy of ancient India; about the physiological and neurological benefits of mindfulness and contemplative practices, such as meditation. And, bit by bit, I noticed myself changing. My brain rewired itself as new ways of thinking were established and I put into practice all that I was learning.

I learned to see, through experience, just how much the negative patterns and outdated mindsets I'd automatically inherited at birth had driven my behaviour and decision-making my entire life. I also started to notice the positive ripple effect that my changing frame of mind and lifestyle habits were having on those around me (family, friends, students), inspiring change in others too. If our mindset is learned, why not change it? Why not learn something else? If we each engaged in some mental spring-cleaning, what might the effect be for humanity as a whole? The possibility was so exciting to me that I dedicated myself to sharing it with the world. Part of what came of that is Jacqui and my film, *The Portal*, and this book.

I met Jacqui a few years into the life of the project when she first joined the film team. Jacqui tends not to be 'part of the system' and likes to think outside the box. It was refreshing; it's rare to find people who aren't conforming to society's norms and are, instead, pushing the boundaries. Her strong affinity with the project stems from her interest in the ways we can deepen the human experience, including meditation. She is passionate about inspiring a shift in people, from their heads to their hearts, and wanted to create an *experience* for the audience and reader instead of the ideas being consumed purely intellectually. In effect, she wanted the audience and reader to *feel* the film and book, so that they would come away in a different state. It was what I had always hoped to achieve with this project.

A new reality

What if a rashi, rather than being viewed as something to avoid, was seen as something positive: a catalyst for change, a trigger to get us on track—or rather, back on track? It could be a prompt for us to dig deep inside ourselves to discover who we really are, what's really important, and what we value most highly. If enough of us looked inwards and used those discoveries to make a personal shift, could we divert the planet from a global rashi? Could we avert centuries—no, millennia—of excess and ignorance, and imminent catastrophe? Could we be the catalyst for change, an evolutionary force that pivots the world to a more enlightened, sustainable future? And if so, what would that enlightened planet look like?

To find the answers, we interviewed more than 300 people, including many who had experienced personal transformation out of crisis. We were moved by countless heart-wrenching stories; the sheer number of people who were willing to open up to us pointed to the urgency for change. We also spoke to philosophers, futurists, scientists and thought leaders at the forefront of technology, innovation and next-paradigm thinking. This book is a collection of nine of the most powerful and insightful of our interviews.

You'll hear from three thought leaders who examine the 'outer view': the global and technological systems we are a part of, the role they play in our current crisis, and a vision of what the future could look like. Daniel Schmachtenberger, an evolutionary philosopher and complex systems strategist; robotics engineer Mikey Siegel; and neuroscientist and artificial intelligence (AI) researcher Dr Julia Mossbridge present the concepts that are emerging from the needs of the time and invite us to consider the bigger questions facing society: How can we transcend the current global paradigm? Could technology become part of the solution? What does it mean to be human?

You'll also see how the factors that may lead us to a global collapse can apply at the personal level (the 'inner view'), through the accounts of six people whose stories unfold episodically through the book. We'll introduce you to Ron 'Booda' Taylor, a retired US serviceman managing post-traumatic stress disorder (PTSD); Due Quach, a Vietnamese refugee who overcame developmental trauma; elite athlete Heather Hennessy, who reinvented herself following a career-ending injury; entrepreneur and neurosurgeon James 'Jim' Doty MD, who had to lose everything to find the meaning of life; human rights expert Amandine Roche, whose commitment to global peace took her on a quest for inner peace; and Rabbi Ronnie Cahana, who found freedom in the confines of personal catastrophe. In an homage to oral storytelling traditions, our six interviewees share their pain and joy in their own words, revealing how they escaped the stranglehold of their past to build lives full of greater connection, love and joy—leading to a desire to make a difference. Their powerful accounts help us understand these questions: What leads to crisis? What is left afterwards? And what is the path that takes us, both personally and as a human race, towards a more enlightened way of life?

But don't think this is your usual new-age book about self-help or personal development. This book is designed to be an emotional and transformative experience no matter where you're at in life: to gently hold your hand as we drift into other people's lives on an intimate exploration of the shifts meditation can bring. And, as we do, a picture begins to emerge of what is possible for each of us—and the planet.

We see this book as a conversation starter, as well as an experience that can lead to a greater sense of connection and community. It's an open invitation to contemplate alternative perspectives and expand your mind about life and possibility. There is also a scattering of quotes throughout the book from spiritual leader Rabbi Ronnie Cahana, whose deeply personal connection to stillness and meditation is shared in Chapter 4. Our hope is to inspire you to make a change in your life, if that's what you need, or to deepen and expand your human experience in some way.

At one point during our interview process, Jacqui was being led by a Bedouin guide on a precarious ride in the dark across the top of Petra back to her hotel. The rocks were slippery and, while the donkey seemed capable enough—and her friendly guide was reassuring—Jacqui held on for dear life. Every time the donkey had to navigate a perilous-looking rock, Jacqui jumped off and clambered down on her own. Finally, as she went to jump off yet again, her Bedouin escort gently pressed her arm to stop her. 'Close your eyes and open your mind,' he urged. It's a message we could all stand to hear more often, and one that we urge you to consider as you read the following pages. There is so much more to life if we remain open to possibility.

We have the capacity as humans to retrain our minds and reconnect to our hearts. We also have the ability to redesign our own and our collective future—if we choose to. But in the face of ubiquitous technology and an ever-increasing pace of life, trembling on the brink of humanity's most daunting challenges, will we adapt quickly enough to make this phase shift? Do we have enough momentum and inspiration to do this together? Come along, join us, and experience for yourself what's waiting on the other side of the portal.

'I woke up in stillness and it was wonderful for me. It was really a great gift from the distortions and the hushings of the exterior world.'

RABBI RONNIE CAHANA

ONE

THE
PROGRAMMING
BEGINS

At birth, and particularly throughout our younger years, we inherit a 'code', an automatically 'downloaded' human operating system, that shapes our reality and influences the way we think and behave in the world.

Tom

Growing up, I attended a Catholic school in a small rural village. Every Friday, the whole school would go to a mass service. Traditionally, you weren't allowed to eat one hour before receiving the Holy Eucharist (a small wafer of bread that Catholics believe is the body of Christ), because the body needs to be pure and clean before consuming it. Before one particular service, I was in the playground biting my nails and the school teacher scolded me in front of everyone for polluting my body before taking the Holy Eucharist. I wasn't allowed to receive the bread that morning. I said a prayer of forgiveness to God that night for my sins, and the shame I had felt out there on the playground lingered for some time.

In the ancient wisdom of Vedic philosophy, which I discovered many years later, there is a concept called *pragya parad*: 'the mistake of the intellect'. It's a rigid mental framework that says 'this is what life is', 'this is who I am' and 'this is who you are'. This way of thinking is passed on through our genetics and our social upbringing, and has a powerful influence over the way we think about ourselves and the world around us. It's like the lens through which we see the world. Pragya parad occurs when this conditioning becomes a mis-take on what's true, and it can have a detrimental impact on our life.

Cultures, religions and the influence of our social environment—including my shaming on the Catholic school playground—are all examples of pragya parad. What is true in one culture or religion can be completely the opposite in another, but the coding can become so deeply ingrained so quickly that we don't realise there are other ways of seeing things. For example, I think I have a certain aesthetic, but if I was born into a Machiguenga tribe in the Peruvian Amazon I might not have that same aesthetic. I wouldn't like that car; I wouldn't like cars at all, right? I would have a totally different set of interests.

I also have a certain set of ethics. I have a certain value system. But, if I was born into a Muslim environment, or a Jewish environment, or any other particular environment, my whole concept of 'me' would be different in the deepest ways.

All of these influences lead to a pattern of thinking about ourselves and life that becomes very repetitive. We typically have 50,000–70,000 thoughts a day, and 85 per cent of these thoughts are the same as the day before, and the day before that. This repetition digs a deep groove in our neural pathways a bit like the Grand Canyon—the longer the water flows along a single path, the more it naturally conforms to that path and carves a deeper groove. It's a catch 22: the more we think that way, the more we think that way.

Most of our lives are spent involved in lots of 'doing', and we never really have the time to pause and reflect deeply on how we got to where we are, what choices we have, and what—or who—is influencing those choices. It's like being on autopilot. There is a word in Sanskrit, *vasanas*, that means patterns of neurological behaviour, like a coding in our software or a tendency of the mind to think in a particular way. This sets our life on a course that can become difficult to change. The interviews in this chapter explore the origins of our automatic programming. Why do we think the way we do—and how does that affect our lives and humanity as a whole?

Jacqui

A small but growing number of people are mapping out a new way forwards, one that isn't bound by the programming prevalent in society today. In this chapter, we introduce two of these progressive thinkers: Daniel Schmachtenberger and Mikey Siegel. Out of the many philosophers, innovators and futurists our team interviewed, why these two?

It was a girlfriend of mine who suggested we contact evolutionary philosopher Daniel Schmachtenberger. Before that, I wasn't familiar with him or his work, but when I checked him out, I could see why she thought he was our guy. Daniel gets called a complex systems strategist, and he is fascinated with civilisations design. He is also a neurohacker who healed the symptoms of his incurable auto-immune neurodegenerative diagnosis through functional medicine (a systems-biology approach to health), and has helped a lot of other people do the same.

If you're not familiar with neurohacking, it's any kind of technology, tool or technique for improving our psychological or neurological function. In ancient times, this involved things like meditation, sweat lodges and psychedelics. Today, neurohacking draws from several fields, including biological psychology, epigenetics, bio/neurofeedback and psychopharmacology (such as smart drugs). People can use these tools and techniques to increase mental performance, decrease anxiety, regulate sleep and shift their consciousness to have more meaningful lives.

Daniel basically spends time trying to unpack the DNA of our societal and biological systems with the desire to help rebuild them from the ground up for an entirely new outcome. He uses the term 'synergistic satisfiers', which describes a solution that manages to satisfy all possible criteria at once. From our perspective, it's a great way of summing up his approach: he's focused on the win-win and all the ways society can evolve to flip from what Daniel calls the current 'win-lose' dynamic. It's an entire rethink and involves asking big, challenging questions. Fortunately, he's a deep thinker and questioner.

Brought up in the Fairfield Iowa community where he attended the world's largest transcendental meditation training centre (Maharishi University), Daniel was home-schooled using facilitated learning, and became especially interested in Eastern philosophy and sciences. Since he was young, Daniel has contemplated humanity and society deeply, and considered how to bust through the normal mental constraints of what's 'possible' in order to go about solving the hard problems we're not good at solving yet. It's a way of thinking and addressing challenges that he was encouraged to do as a child. He believes that we're currently experiencing a global destabilisation in which things are simultaneously getting better and worse at the same time, and that a phase shift is imminent.

Daniel is involved in a lot of cutting-edge projects and can be a hard guy to get hold of. But no matter how close we were to filming or to locking off commitments from all our participants, I knew we wanted him for this project. After six weeks, we got the call. I'll never forget it. I was in the United States driving back from my meeting with Booda; Tom was in Sydney, Daniel in California. Rain was lashing the car and I was exhausted. I had to stop and it was even hard to hear Tom and Daniel speaking.

The whole call was utterly fascinating, but it was the last thing Daniel said that particularly struck us: an idea that felt so meaningful given all the doomsday scenarios with which we had been presented. He suggested that we invite readers and viewers to imagine their personal vision of what an enlightened future would look like. Essentially, what he was talking about was our audience engaging in a global visualisation exercise. Many of us are familiar with the concepts of visualisation and manifesting, and the power of the mind to bring things into physical form, but imagine the collective power if everyone who read this book or saw the film did that. What if seven billion people did that? Our skin tingled with possibility.

Daniel traverses big ideas quickly and with precision. He has a wonderful way of explaining how things got to be the way they are by giving tangible examples so that you end up feeling like you understand the inner workings of the world. It's part of the way he helps people see the idea of creating a world based on a different set of principles as something actually achievable.

In the personal accounts in this chapter, we step back into Booda's, Due's, Heather's, Jim's and Amandine's childhoods, and get a sense of how they became the people they are today. What Daniel does, over the course of the book, is deconstruct aspects of the equivalent global process. Basically, a bit of a civilisation backstory. Ultimately, he suggests that our current predicament is a developmental stage and a part of evolution. We've found it extraordinarily helpful to think of what's going on as part of a process because, when we understand that, it's easier to remain hopeful and not be too overwhelmed to actively participate as an individual in getting to the next stage.

So you, me and humanity—we're all experiencing growing pains.

The truth is that civilisations have always faced challenges, and they haven't necessarily come through them (an idea that Daniel will bring us back to). One view that comes up frequently is that the challenges we currently face were all created by humans, so humans are the key to finding the solutions.

Mikey Siegel is well known for the catchphrase 'We create what we are'. I find this saying so simple but incredibly fundamental, as it acts as a guiding force in life.

I initially heard about Mikey's work in the book *Stealing Fire: How Silicon Valley, the Navy SEALs, and Maverick Scientists Are Revolutionizing the Way We Live and Work*, from Flow Genome Project's Steven Kotler and Jamie Wheal. I love learning about high performance, human optimisation and brainhacking, and so on, so at the time, it was the most exhilarating book that I had come across. These guys are leading the way in 'flow' research, also known as being 'in the zone': a state of optimal experience. The book featured numerous incredible case studies that make it worth checking out, including Mikey's on the work he does in transformational technology development: a field now known as 'enlightenment engineering'. He explores things like how to increase group connection and coherence, and how to 'hack' your own state of consciousness using cutting-edge technological tools. He also lectures in 'Technology as a tool for transformation and flourishing' at Stanford University, where he's involved in creating a new curriculum at the intersection of engineering, meditation and contemplative science as part of their WellnessEd division.

I asked the team to track him down; we needed to speak to this guy.

To me, Mikey is kind of an everyman. He's got an unassuming yet intellectual surfie vibe (I don't know if he actually surfs). He's spiritual but not esoteric, and is a quintessential optimist. I was excited to meet him.

We'd previously had a bit of a pocket-dial incident during which I got to listen to some Burning Man prep-talk between Mikey and his friend ahead of the upcoming event. Burning Man is a huge annual arts and music gathering where 70,000 people converge for seven days in the middle of the Nevada desert. Mikey wasn't going, although he'd been in the past to road-test his prototype 'heart cart' by giving people at Burning Man the opportunity to sync up heart rates for increased coherence with a partner. But between the pocket-dial and some jetlag/poor sleep management on my part, we hadn't really had the connection I'd hoped for ahead of our meeting.

We were a little behind schedule, but happy with how the interview was going. Then, midway through, Mikey unexpectedly turned the spotlight back on us and said extremely earnestly: 'And you, I'm looking at you, the creators of this project ... your intention, your ideas, your biases, your judgement ... all of that will be transmitted through this film and book and will impact every single person who watches it.'

Gulp.

It hit home. It's a huge responsibility, and a statement like that stops you in your tracks. Where are my biases coming out in my work and life? Is my intention clear? I'm always focused on self-development, but what are other steps I could take to ensure that the work I'm involved in is free of the unconscious aspects of me? 'We create what we are' has become one of my mantras—an idea so important that I aim to have it consistently present in my awareness to inspire in me my very best.

Awareness: it's the first step to change.

the outer view

Who am I, actually?

DANIEL SCHMACHTENBERGER, EVOLUTIONARY PHILOSOPHER
AND GLOBAL SYSTEMS STRATEGIST

It's important when we think about civilisation and its curve moving forwards that we look back at previous civilisations and realise that one thing that they all had in common—the Roman Empire, the Byzantine, Mayan, Aztec, et cetera—is that they all collapsed. None of those empires exist today in the form they were in at their peak. It's actually the precedent that civilisations have a life cycle, and that they reach the end of their lives because whatever the design parameters were that made them successful encountered something they couldn't handle, or there was something self-terminating (anti-evolutionary) in the system itself, like non-renewable use of resources in their environment. So it's the precedent that civilisations collapse.

The tricky difference right now is that, for the first time, we don't have local civilisations. We have a globally interconnected civilisation. So collapse would actually be an existential scenario.

Throughout history, the existence of agriculture has led to environmental damage. We've had scenarios where escalating power led to wars that created collapse (of a civilisation, society, or system), or where the population outstripped the resource capacity of an area. We've just never had a situation where the environmental collapse would be global, or where the wars had enough technological power on all sides to actually threaten the existence of humankind. We've never had the technological capacity to actually destroy the planet's ability to sustain human existence. We've also never had the technological capacity to create a world of abundance in perpetuity for everybody, and that is really the kind of fork in the road that we're at.

As a child, I started contemplating what life would be like on an enlightened planet. The reason why I like thinking about an enlightened planet is because it frees us up to imagine a different world 'system' and society beyond the otherwise conditioned ways of thinking about human limitation. So on an enlightened planet, how would the beings relate to their own emotions? How would they relate to communication and to the other types of species that inhabit their planet with them? How would they manage their differences? How would they relate to their own thoughts, their desires, their sexuality, all of that? What would it take for a planet to really function well, for its inhabitants to be fulfilled and have the highest quality of life?

These aren't the types of questions many of us are brought up to ask. We've been taught to think and behave in a particular way, which often leads to statements like, 'Oh, humans couldn't be that way,' and, 'We could never do that here,' et cetera. Our current education system was developed in the Industrial Age to make people into good industrial agents. It is not optimised to help people figure out what is worthwhile, what they are passionate about, what they value or what they love. The current system has been optimised for preparing people for the economy. This Industrial Age mindset has led to people being parts of an industrial machine.

When a kid asks, 'Why is the sky blue?' 'Why does fire hurt?' 'Where do we go after death?', we don't have good answers, so we just don't answer them—we don't facilitate. These kids are then forced to be interested in stuff that they aren't interested in at all. We break their interest in life that way; we program them for failure.

When we start to realise that most of what we think is 'us' is actually programmed into us via other people and the system itself (religion, language, culture, society), and that core parts of our identity would be different if we happened to have been born in a different place or had a different experience, we start asking, 'Well, who am I, actually?'

Our internal operating system

MIKEY SIEGEL, ROBOTICS ENGINEER AND TRANSFORMATIVE TECHNOLOGY DEVELOPER

This is a unique time for our species. If you look around, unlike a few thousand years ago, nearly every single global crisis, nearly every major issue that we face as a species, is a human-generated problem. There are so many global issues that we can see at the surface: environmental problems, political issues, issues of resource distribution, you name it. But I believe that underneath every one of these issues is human pain and human suffering. So the problem that we're facing is a human problem.

One of my favourite quotes is the first line of the UNESCO Constitution from the United Nations (UN), which says, 'Since wars begin in the minds of men, it's in the minds of men that the defences of peace must be constructed.'[2] For me, what this quote is pointing to is that it's the human mind that is creating the conflict that we exist in: that our perception, our beliefs, our state of consciousness, our rejection of ourselves and the world around us, is the cause of the wars, the violence and the conflict that exists.

When we're born, whether we like it or not, we take on the beliefs, the ideas, the assumptions, the worldview of our parents, and their parents, and their parents, and the community and culture around us. It's like a program that is downloaded the moment we're born and gets deeper and deeper as we go through school, as we watch TV, as we become ensconced in society, and as we learn to participate in the game-playing that we see and experience all around us.

The simple truth is that this program is outdated. And not only is it outdated, but this program is killing us. It's killing our planet. It's causing us to kill each other and it's perpetuating a culture of greed, of hatred, of violence.

We are also born into this idea that there is some set of circumstances, something that we can change or configure about the world around us, that will ultimately make us complete. So, we go about our lives trying to fix and change and reject the way things are—trying to fix, change and reject the way *we* are—so that we can finally be okay.

I started my journey as an engineer. (Since I was a little kid, I've been building stuff and taking stuff apart.) I ended up studying robotics through graduate school. As much as I loved what I was doing, and as much as when I looked around I had everything that I wanted in life, I had to come to a pretty tough realisation: I still felt like crap. I had anxiety, I felt disconnected, I felt this sort of constant existential angst. My emotional experience was squashed into a flat line. And what I embarked upon was, from an engineering perspective, the journey to understand human happiness. The journey to understand why, when everything around me seemed so good, I could feel so bad. And what I discovered was myself.

What I realised was that, as an engineer, I was only looking at half of the equation, the external world, and that there was this entire universe inside me—my thoughts, my beliefs, my emotions—that was, by far, the biggest determining factor in how I experienced reality and how I acted in the world.

This is my code, my 'operating system'. And I realised that this operating system needed to be upgraded. And what I began to do was take an engineering approach to upgrading my internal operating system. I started exploring meditation, going on retreats, travelling to India, looking into psychedelics—anything that I could find to support my transformation. What I found was profound.

First, I discovered that we can radically change our experience of reality by upgrading our internal operating system. But another thing I found was even more important: that my internal operating system influences everything I do in this world, and everything I create as a maker, as an engineer, as an inventor. And I realised that was true for every single person on this planet. Then I knew that I had my mission. It was very clear: as an engineer, the only problem worth solving was upgrading the human operating system and elevating consciousness.

We have many different approaches to elevating consciousness and supporting wellbeing: there's engineering, technology and science— and there is meditation. These two spheres—the scientific and the spiritual—seem to be in conflict, but I realised that this was an artificial divide. It was a cultural relic. There's absolutely no reason why I couldn't, as an engineer, begin to work on and develop new technologies that had the exact same function, and the exact same purpose, as meditation techniques and spiritual traditions have had for thousands of years. We consider water, food and shelter to be basic human needs, and now, access to information is being recognised as a basic human need. I believe that access to tools that can support psychological, emotional and spiritual wellbeing should be considered another basic human need.

And so my purpose, discovered through these years of exploration, has been the application of science and technology towards the uplifting of humanity, towards supporting human wellbeing and towards collective human awakening.

It's not just about feeling better. It's actually about being more accurate. It's about operating more effectively. When political systems, educational systems, economic systems, scientific and technological systems, when our human systems are operating from this old programming, they're perpetuating old, destructive ideas.

The most important problem we can solve right now is how to upgrade the human operating system. And the single most important thing we can do to support humanity is to fix the bugs in our outdated programming.

the inner view: part 1

BOODA | Violence was part of my DNA

RON 'BOODA' TAYLOR, RETIRED US ARMY SERGEANT

My earliest memory is being in kindergarten at Fort Hood, Texas. We lived on base at the time, but my dad was hardly around. I remember he had this big, round, brown Smokey the Bear-type hat on his dresser, so I knew he was a drill sergeant. He was gone for a few years, and when he came back home from Germany, we moved into a different, nicer home. Years later, I learned that my dad had been kicked out of the army for dealing drugs.

I don't even know the job that he had after the army, but I think he was driving trucks at one point, and a school bus. Again, he wasn't home much and, when he was home, everybody was afraid to be around him. He would sleep (and you couldn't interrupt his sleep), or if he was watching TV, you had to watch what he was watching. You couldn't make any noise. You couldn't eat his food; he had his food, we had our food. If you touched something of his, you got beat bad.

One night, he and my mom got into this huge fight, like an actual physical fight. They would fight all the time, but never in front of us. This time it went from the bedroom to the living room, then out into the driveway. It was horrible. Dad came back into the house, grabbed his stuff and left. The next day after that altercation, he came back while my mom was at work and packed up everything in the house as we were sitting there. He unplugged the TV, just cleared the place out and left. He didn't say anything to us.

For me, my dad was everything. No matter what you said, my dad was God's gift to humankind, so when he left I blamed my mom, like it was her fault. That's when I really noticed the decline. We didn't have money for anything. My mom would hide from the landlord because she couldn't pay the rent. I remember our lights being turned off, our water getting turned off. We would hook a water hose up to the next-door neighbour's house and run it through the bathroom window to fill the tub and fill up all the pots and pans and cups, so we'd have drinking water. We burned candles because we didn't have any electricity.

That was just normal; we didn't realise how poor we were and how much we were struggling. We would come home from school and there wouldn't be anything to eat in the house. I got free lunch at school and I would put food in my pockets so that I could feed my family. I would jump into the trash cans outside Dunkin' Donuts to pull out day-old doughnuts, then I'd blow off the coffee grounds. That's what we ate for dinner. Or we would go through the dumpsters outside Burger King and Jack in the Box, brushing cigarette butts off discarded food. My brother and I would steal food out of the grocery store. I mean, we were children, so we'd steal chips and cookies and things like that. One time, we got caught and my mom was embarrassed. Honestly, we were hungry. The store didn't know that. The cops didn't. No one cared.

Finally, my uncle (he's my godfather) and my grandmother packed us up and we moved to Beaumont, Texas, to live with my grandparents. I was about 11 or 12 at the time. We were there for maybe six months when my mom's lifestyle took a turn for the worse. She fell in with childhood friends and you could tell something was wrong. They looked like bums. If you know anything about junkies, they don't understand that they're junkies. They think they're perfectly normal. They come around and think they're talking normal, think they're acting normal, but they're not. They're twitching and asking a lot of questions really fast. As a child, I'd never seen it before. It was an uneasy feeling. I was like, *These people are weird*. My mom was on drugs again, though I didn't know that at the time. It was more than my grandparents were willing to accept. They put us out onto the street.

We moved into the housing projects of Beaumont—the 'hood'. It was a small town, but they had huge crime, a lot of violence. I'm talking about the '90s, when gang violence was high and everybody sold drugs. You might not have wanted to be in a gang, but you were going to be in one. You didn't have a choice; it was the environment we were in. What are you going to do? Fall in. I knew I was meant to be more than that, but I didn't see a way out.

I had to be tough all the time. If you didn't fight, you'd get picked on. Whether you're beat up or not, you gotta fight. Somebody told my mom that me and my brother were getting jumped or getting beat up at the pool. The next thing you know, she comes flying through the park like a raging bull, wielding an axe-handle and a pistol. The park cleared out quick. Violence was just a part of my DNA.

I used to break into houses—my mom doesn't know this stuff, so she's about to find out. I'd break in houses, break in cars, break in hotels, stores, you name it. I held people at gunpoint. We used to rob the poor pizza guy. We'd call for a pizza and he would show up and we would rob him and steal everything else in his car. I think stealing was why I got fired from my job at the Hilton Hotel restaurant. I was stealing all kinds of stuff. Same thing at a restaurant I worked at as a dishwasher. People would leave tips and I would go around bussing the tables and taking the tips.

At first, seeing all the easy money that drug dealers made, I thought I wanted to get in on that. One of my mom's friends was a known drug dealer, so I talked to him and said: 'I wanna get in the game. What do I need to do? I want to work for you.'

And he cussed me out. He went off on me, saying, 'I don't ever wanna hear you say that stupid shit again. This ain't what you need to do. You don't want to get into this life. Trust me. It's not what you think it is. I'd rather give you the money to make sure you don't get into the lifestyle than to teach you how to get into the lifestyle.'

So, he gave me 20 bucks. Later that night, he was killed in a bar … stabbed in the heart in a dispute over a woman.

Dead or in jail—that was the theme.

As my grandmother was passing away in hospital, she made us all promise that we would make something out of ourselves. My grandmother was everything to me. When I was little, that's how my mom punished me: I'd get in trouble and she'd say I couldn't visit my grandmother. I would purposely walk the long way to go see her in the morning before I went to school, just so I could spend 30 minutes or an hour with her. I lost it when she died. I didn't cry in front of anybody, though. I held it in. I'm the strong one, you know? I just kind of lost my conscience at that point, and that's when I really started rebelling hard.

I ended up in court because I ran a light and got a ticket. The judge said to me, 'Isn't your grandmother Martha? You're Martha May's boy.'

I started crying on the spot. She said to me, 'What are you going to do with yourself? Because if you come in my courtroom again, if I have to see you again, I'm not going to have any mercy.' She was going off on me, asking, 'Have you ever thought about joining the military? Doing something with yourself?'

At the time I had never thought of it, but I didn't want to be a statistic. I didn't want to die or go to jail, so I took her advice and I went and talked to the army recruiter.

I was 17, and my mom had to sign a waiver so the recruiters could take me to Fort Polk, Louisiana, to see an artillery show. They were shooting all kinds of guns. The recruiter was like, 'You like guns?' I said, 'I love guns.' So we watched the shooting and he asked, 'Is this what you want to do?' I'm like, *Hell yes, I could do this every day.*

In many ways, joining the military saved my life. Except now I have seen not only the horrors of the man-on-the-street violence, but the horrors of violence on a global stage, too.

'We humans are so easily corruptible,

and we're so frail and susceptible

to things that are our opposites.

We have that component in us

not to grow. I look to find the impetus

to continue; our own small limitations

shouldn't stop our growth.'

RABBI RONNIE CAHANA

DUE | They brought their trauma with them

DUE QUACH, SOCIAL ENTREPRENEUR AND REFUGEE

When I was a baby we were living in Ho Chi Minh City, in the Chinese area. It was at the end of the Vietnam War, and my parents saw neighbours taken away in the night to concentration camps. Some never came back alive. Around that time, there was a war breaking out between Vietnam and Cambodia, and China, being an ally of Cambodia, actually invaded northern Vietnam.

There was a strong message sent to everyone of Chinese ancestry that Chinese people might not be welcome in Vietnam anymore. My parents decided to escape and try to bring my brother and me to America. They hired a boat from smugglers and, in the middle of the night, we got onto the boat in the Mekong Delta. I was about six months old. My brother was a little bit older. Many people on the boat ran out of food. There were storms and the boat was over capacity. It took over a week of drifting for us to make it to a refugee camp.

Conditions in the camp were terrible. Tropical diseases were rampant and every day children and elderly people died. I caught several diseases and barely survived. We were in the camp over a year before we were accepted to emigrate to America.

My parents brought their fear and their trauma to America with them.

My earliest memories are of the dangerous neighbourhood in Philadelphia where we were resettled. Life at home was one way, and life outside of home was a different way. It was almost like travelling between two different countries every day.

When we were growing up, it was the '80s and there was more violence, more gangs, a lot of crack dealers. It was pretty much in your face. My dad was nearly robbed several times coming home from work. One time, when we were kids, I was maybe five years old, my cousin and older brother were about seven, they were jumped by kids down the street for being different. My cousin had to be hospitalised. It was not an easy place to grow up in and feel safe.

When I was about eight years old, my parents bought a takeout restaurant. They had saved up the money, and it was easier to run one business than work several jobs to pay the rent. My grandmother was also becoming more and more mentally ill, and my parents needed to work from home to take care of her. They got a good deal on the takeout, but it was in a neighbourhood that was quite violent.

When we opened the takeout, we realised that not everyone wanted us there. People used to call just to say ridiculously awful things—horribly racist things. They didn't care if a child answered the phone. Some of them threatened to kill us for no reason. That's when I was like, 'Wow, there are people in this neighbourhood who really don't want us here because of the colour of our skin.'

The kids we played with in our block started throwing rocks at the window. My dad had found a bike at the junkyard and fixed it up for me. They actually stole the bike and destroyed it. It was really hurtful that the people you thought were your friends could just turn on you.

Asian refugees just weren't welcome. Even though the neighbourhood was diverse, people were still hostile towards those from the outside. One of the first things my dad did was install bulletproof plexiglass in the restaurant. It dawned on me then that we could actually get robbed by people with guns.

People really did shoot guns into the takeout, too. I used to find bullets and wondered how miraculous it was that we never got shot. Because it was so dangerous, my dad had to put bars on all the windows, and he put gates on the backyard so no one could come in. But that also meant no one could go out. It was like a prison.

It was especially hard because my grandmother was mentally ill and needed full-time care. Sometimes she would have an episode where she would chase us with knives. It was terrifying. My parents couldn't put her in a nursing home because she couldn't speak English and people couldn't communicate with her. It was better to have her at home, where they could at least talk to her in her native language.

After the takeout opened, my parents needed me to help run the store and take orders while they took care of my grandmother. I saw things that were just terrible. Quite a few of our women customers were addicted to drugs, and they would come in with their babies and try to trade their food stamps or use their food stamps to buy cigarettes instead of feeding their children. The babies would just cry and cry. I felt terrible for them.

My parents would keep the takeout open until midnight or so for anyone wanting late dinners. Gangs used to come in, rob people, beat people up. I got used to hearing people fighting in the restaurant or cursing my parents out, or kids crying—that became part of our tapestry of sounds.

In the beginning, I would always be hyper-alert and, if something happened, I would go downstairs and offer to call the police. But then it became so common that I was like, *My parents probably have the hang of this now, and they know enough English to call 911. If it's super serious, they'll come and get me.*

Most of the time, things de-escalated. The person would calm down and leave the store. But once, when I was in junior high, a customer was shot in the head leaving the store. I think he was part of a gang. He had robbed customers the night before, and he robbed the wrong person. So they put out a vendetta on him. When he came back to our store, word got out and they assassinated him. After the authorities took him away, they left the clean-up to us. I will never forget the amount of blood and brains we had to wash away. I learned that there's a dangerous code. If you don't mess with the code, you're okay. But if you mess with the code—if you mess with the gangs, if you get involved—you're in trouble.

There was a crime ring in Philadelphia where Asian people robbed Asian people. My parents were very paranoid about becoming victims in any way. Several times, people with guns were waiting to rob our takeout restaurant when my dad closed it, and a neighbour would call and say: 'Don't come out. There are people outside waiting to hurt you.' It wasn't a great experience, but we also learned eventually that we had a lot of wonderful neighbours who would look out for us.

Growing up, my brother and I kind of never knew who we were. I used to be like, 'What does being Asian mean?' Am I white or am I black? I was trying to be black, listening to LL Cool J, MC Hammer, Salt-N-Pepa, trying to learn how to rap, trying to learn how to do the running man. My parents had a lot of rules about what boys could do versus what girls could do. My dad saw me waving 'hi' to a classmate who was a boy. He was just a friend. But my dad said, 'Girls should not wave hello to boys because they'll think that you like them. You have to be careful not to send hints to boys. Let them wave to you first.' I was like, 'Seriously? This is bizarre.' That kind of thing happened a lot.

During my freshman year of high school, I was chosen by my teacher to be one of the representatives of the school at the World Youth Summit for Gifted Education. It was going to be in Toronto. My dad said to me, 'You're a young girl. You're not allowed to leave home without your parents going with you. We obviously can't go with you, so can you ask your teacher to send your brother in your place?' He thought this was transferable, that an honour that was given to me was something I could pass on to my older brother. I said, 'It doesn't work that way, Dad. Either I go or I don't go and they pick someone else. I can't nominate my older brother.' Even my brother was embarrassed.

Because my parents couldn't really understand English, I had to do a lot of translating for them. I could see that they really wanted us to assimilate. They didn't want to teach us Vietnamese or Chinese because they didn't want us to speak with an accent. They wanted us to make them proud. They came to America so that we could have a better future, so they always pushed me to study and reminded me that, in Vietnam, I wouldn't have had access to good schools. That was fine with me, because I loved learning. It was my escape.

My brother and I ended up at a parochial (Catholic) school because he had gone to the local elementary school and, in first grade, came home with a broken arm. My mom didn't understand what had happened to him, how his arm could have been broken at school without anyone telling her or treating him for it. They asked around the Vietnamese community and found a priest who said he could help get us into a local parochial school and help us get scholarships because we were low-income refugees. It meant that my parents had to work a lot harder to pay the portion that they had to pay, but they felt it was worth it.

When I started school there, I had developmental challenges. When we were in the refugee camps, I nearly died from different diseases. I'm not sure if it was that or the period of malnutrition that we went through that affected my brain. Any six-month-old baby who doesn't eat for two or three days is probably affected. My kindergarten teacher thought that I might be dumb—literally dumb—or deaf, because

I didn't know how to talk. She wanted to send me off to learn sign language. But I had gone to preschool, so the preschool teacher vouched for me, saying that I could clearly make sense of instructions and had a normal intelligence.

The school decided to let me stay and try English as a second language and give me speech therapy. Slowly, by second grade, once I learned how to read, English started making more sense and I could actually, with the help of the speech therapist, pronounce the words correctly. I became a good student.

I went to a magnet (specialist) high school in Philadelphia called Central. After my freshman year, they came out with class rankings. I didn't think that I'd be more than average, but I came out at number two. *Was there a mistake?* My counsellor assured me, 'No, you're really ranked number two. This is not a mistake.' That's when people started telling me I might be able to get into Harvard.

Then in the spring of our junior year, there was a special assembly where they gave out college book awards and they gave the Harvard book award to me. I went to see my counsellor afterwards and he told me, 'I nominated you for this book award so that you understand that you should apply to Harvard.' I was like, 'Seriously? I can't imagine that.' He said, 'You have a decent shot. I can help you get fee waivers. It won't cost you anything.' He knew we were low income.

I went home and I told my parents and they asked, 'What's Harvard?' I had to explain to them that it was the top school in the country, and they said, 'Oh, really? Why would it take you?' I explained what my counsellor had said about the fee waivers, that I could apply and just see what happened.

They were like, 'Well, you know, you're a girl. We've told you before that you should be staying at home. You really can't leave home for college.' I said, 'But this is the best school. You really wouldn't let me go?' They said, 'You probably won't get in. But if you go, you have to become a doctor.' They put this condition on me to be a doctor from Harvard because it would be so prestigious. I crossed my fingers and promised. Ultimately, it was a promise I never kept.

I applied, and in the fall of my senior year, I got accepted. Everyone was blown away. And I couldn't help seeing it as my golden ticket out of the ghetto.

HEATHER | Generational patterns of abuse

HEATHER HENNESSY, FORMER US NATIONAL TRACK
ATHLETE AND SPORTS TV PRESENTER

From an early age, it felt like I had this sort of calling. Like I already knew my life story in some way. And then, as I got into sports, I thought my impact in life was going to be through my running—that I would be able to help people and inspire people through running track.

When I was in third grade I remember winning a race, which felt amazing, and I remember thinking, *Wow, I'm fast. I got this.* In sixth grade, the school had this race to determine the fastest kid in the school. It was me and this other guy who were the two really athletic ones. We raced and I beat him, and I felt so proud of that.

I was fairly young when I knew things in my family were dysfunctional. For sure, fourth grade, fifth grade, sixth grade were the years when it started to make sense to me that things were really bad. It was a constant state of chaos in my household, but the most painful thing to watch was the way my dad directed his anger at my mother. He put her down a lot; it was a kind of verbal abuse situation.

There were days when family life was fun, and then days that were really dark. You were just kind of always walking on eggshells, not knowing what you were going to get. It depended on what mood my dad woke up in, whether it was going to be a good day or not. There was never one normal day.

I started to hear my dad with other women, talking to other women, and I began to piece that together and understand what it meant. So that was confusing to know he was having an affair behind my mother's back. I was holding in a lot of anger towards him about that. There was no one to really talk to. Not knowing what my mom knew, seeing what was going on with my dad, I felt somehow caught in the middle. That's when I started having stomach aches. I now realise it was the result of stress because of what I was living around and witnessing. I just remember complaining to my mom and my grandma that my stomach hurt. I wasn't able to verbalise my true feelings because that would upset my dad.

Growing up with brothers and my dad, I naturally became a tomboy. My dad pushed us all into sports. He had been a track runner at Rice University on a full scholarship; running was a huge part of his life. Everything in our house revolved around success in sports. So I became really competitive; maybe I partly got that from my dad. My mom was an athlete too, so they were both super competitive. When I did well in a race, I saw my dad happy, and that made me want to do well—to keep the peace.

My parents divorced when I was 13. In the lead-up to that, things had escalated. My dad had addiction problems and his own demons that he was struggling with. I think that was something he took out on my mom, not being self-aware enough to understand what a healthy relationship was. So eventually, my mom left my dad—but then I was stuck with him, and he began to take a lot of his anger out on me. We had a lot of arguments. That was challenging because I was trying to find my voice but I would get matched back by a father who was calling me names, putting me down and telling me I was wrong for feeling what I felt.

At some point, I started to get angry back at him. I had held things in for so long as a young girl and I'd had enough. I finally thought, *No, I'm going to stand up to you.* And there were times when I did that and he slapped me across the face.

But when I was doing well in track, he would be happy. Track and sports were the only areas where we could come together and get along. So that was something sports gave me: a relationship with my father. It also gave me a confidence boost. I was a blonde, skinny female who didn't look very powerful, but I had a big heart and a competitor's soul, and on the track I was able to show that and shock people. It was very empowering, like, *Don't judge me for how I look.*

At that time in my life, it was all about having a vision of what I was going to do to make my running career happen. There was only so much I could do to get away from where I was. I didn't have any control over my environment. I knew that if I spent every day training and working hard, that was going to be my ticket to freedom. So, my goal became to win a scholarship to college using sports. I just put that in my mind and focused on what I had to do to make it happen. At that age, I had no idea that I would go on to be as successful as I was in track.

During all those years, my mom had been the one stable force in the house. Even when my dad was up and down, she was always trying to hold things together. So to have her leave was terrifying in so many ways. When she moved out, it was one of the scariest, hardest times of my life. I did a pretty good job of hiding that, but during eighth grade and my freshman year of high school, I spent almost every night crying. There was a period when I didn't eat; I was running a lot and lost a lot of weight. My mom started to get worried about me, because I went from 120 pounds to, like, 90 pounds. I had no appetite. I think a lot of that was an emotional response to not knowing how to cope with the trauma.

During that time, my life was a little scattered. I shared an apartment with Mom for a while. Sometimes I was at my dad's, which was never stable. I was always jumping around, just trying to find my place within my family, and then my place within my life. Sports gave me some form of stability and structure. The team became my second family.

My family situation motivated me. In a way, it was my fuel. I think my coaches thought I was crazy because I trained so hard. They would try to kick me out, and I was like, no, I'm just going to stay here. I'm not going to go home. I don't want to go home. But I also felt like I had to be there for my brothers and, being the eldest, I felt that I had to play a role in the family to support them and help make things easier on them.

My father's behaviour taught me how these patterns, generational patterns of abuse, just get passed down. He grew up with an abusive father himself, then went on to treat us the same way. I would eventually have to break the pattern if I didn't want to inflict it on my own family.

JIM | The monkey we put on our back

JAMES R. DOTY MD, NEUROSURGEON AND NEUROSCIENTIST

Some people find the ability to be vulnerable—to show your true self, to care—challenging. In the context of my job as a neurosurgeon, I can't be operating on somebody and be vulnerable to their humanity. If I do that, then I can't save them. I can't do what's necessary, because I'm so distracted by who they are in their humanity, and what it means if I fail.

So you have to be able to be absolutely focused, but only on the task at hand. Unfortunately, you have to completely objectify the situation, which separates you from them.

I had an experience with my own daughter, who had injured herself—she'd ruptured a disc in her back. She wouldn't let anyone operate on her, except for me. You would not do that normally, but she was insistent. Even though this was my daughter, who I love dearly, I had to be a surgeon for her that day, before I was her father. I did the operation and I was able to do that with complete separation, with detachment, which some people would not be able to do at all.

She did perfectly fine and all was well, but this ability to go from those different positions of deep, immense caring and empathy, to one of objectivity, many find very hard. For some, they can't focus on doing their job and so they separate themselves, but it becomes a constant separation. They become unable to separate from the pain, or the emotion. Instead, they just learn to never have that emotion, never allow it to surface, never to sit with it—and they lose. They lose so much and so many of the lessons life has for us, because they're not living anymore.

I used to do that as a kid, too, and it's certainly a skill that I had to learn. It took time to retrain my mind and break the pattern. But when I did learn it, it changed my life.

Oftentimes, there is an assumption because of my position or perhaps the way that I talk that my background is one of affluence and privilege. They don't know that I grew up in poverty. They don't know that my father was an alcoholic. They don't know that my mother was chronically depressed and attempted suicide multiple times. I was lost and angry and had immense despair.

Throughout my entire childhood, we were on public assistance. We had been evicted multiple times for non-payment of rent. I was in constant fear, thinking, *Are we going to be evicted tomorrow? Will there be something to eat when I get home? Do I have shoes? Are they worn out?* For a while, I was an explorer scout. At that time—it was the '60s—they had different specialties, so I was in the law enforcement for a while, and then I was in medical. As a medical explorer, we would pack Christmas baskets or Thanksgiving baskets for the poor. Later, I would be at home and we'd receive one.

My father would go on alcoholic binges and we would never know what was going to happen. We could have a week or a month of seeming 'normality', and then he would just not show up. Or he would not show up when he was supposed to, then show up much later, drunk and angry. We'd be sleeping and suddenly there would be pounding on the door and screaming from our father demanding to be let in. Our mother was so chronically depressed she wouldn't get out of bed to even answer the door. Usually it was me who would have to deal with him because my older brother would go into his room and cry.

I was often so focused on my own suffering that I couldn't look out at other people and be kind to them. I had a lot of anger, hostility, fear and anxiousness in me. When others looked at me, they could see that. I didn't feel I had a future, or opportunities. At least not the ones I wished for, so I gave up. Once you give up, you have nothing to lose. And I was on the road to becoming a juvenile delinquent.

Don't get me wrong; it wasn't like I was carrying a gun or anything. I'd break into the school, vandalise things, steal things, but never on a major level. They were just stupid things you do when you have too much time and no direction. I remember one time we were stealing gas from some car. I had misgivings about it, thinking, *Geez, I don't want to take all this person's gas.* This was really wrong and I knew it was wrong. The guy I was doing it with, he fundamentally was a criminal. I was just doing it to steal gas, but people start judging you.

I used to have this Stingray bicycle, and it had a banana seat and a high bar in the back that you could lean against. I had worked delivering newspapers and bought that bicycle, so it was a treasure. Riding it was a way that I could escape for a while: just run out, jump on my bicycle and zoom along.

In those moments of childhood, freedom was being able to close your eyes, feel the wind blow on your face and the warmth of the sun and, for a very brief period, think about nothing else, because nothing else mattered. There was no anger. There was no hostility. There was no fear. There was no anxiousness. I was able to simply be.

One day, I rode out to an area that I never really went to and there was a magic shop. I loved magic and doing magic tricks at the time, so I went in and there was a woman seated on a shag carpet, reading a paperback novel. She had glasses on with a chain that went around her neck. She had grey hair and was overweight—an Earth Mother type of woman.

She looked up at me and had the most radiant smile. We've all met people who, when they look at you, you just feel warmth and love and a sense that they're not judging you at all. That was the feeling I got from her.

She took her glasses off and looked at me, straight in the eye, like no other adult had done before.

'I'm Ruth,' she said. 'What's your name?'

'I'm Jim,' I said. I then asked her about some things related to magic and she looked at me and said, 'I don't know anything about it. This is my son's store. I'm just here because he's running an errand.'

Because of my background—actually, my fear and shame—I never shared my story with the people I met, but we got chatting and, with her, it was different. I actually answered her questions and some of them were really penetrating. I answered them honestly, which I would never normally have done. At the end of about 15 or 20 minutes, she looked right into my eyes and said, 'You know, I think I could teach you something that could change your life.'

Now, I was 12 years old and I didn't know what that meant, but I listened. She said, 'I'm here for another six weeks and if you come in every day and spend an hour or two with me, you'll see what you can learn.' She seemed really nice, and she showed me respect and treated me with dignity. Being in her company made me feel happier. Strangely, I felt loved by her, which was weird considering I'd only just met her.

Summer in Lancaster, California, was a hot and boring experience. The apartment complex I lived in was surrounded by empty, dusty streets and tumbleweed with an abandoned car or piece of derelict machinery here and there. I had nothing else to do, so at 10 am every day, I would get on my Stingray and ride over to the magic shop. Then whenever I would leave Ruth's, I would practise what she taught me and come back and review it with her the next day.

The first thing she taught me was how to just sit and relax. That sounds easy enough, but I wasn't sure if I'd ever been relaxed; my home environment wasn't really conducive to being relaxed. But it wasn't until she made me go through every muscle group and consciously think about every muscle relaxing that I realised how tense I actually was.

I felt so angry and hopeless all the time in response to what was going on in my life that I was holding immense tension in my muscles. It took 10 days of working with Ruth and going home and practising every night for me to be able to relax my entire body.

She assured me that it was a very powerful thing to be able to do, and that it would change everything. At the time, I didn't really know what she was talking about; this was before the terms 'mindfulness' or 'meditation' were regularly used, or before the concept of neuroplasticity existed. This was 1968. So I have to imagine that this woman, in some way, was related to all that was happening in the '60s, with some background in Eastern philosophy and religion, because she understood, intuitively, the concepts of mindfulness and meditation, and the idea that you could change your own brain.

I loved the quiet and calm at the back of the shop. It was a total contrast to the constant noise, TV and shouting at my place. And I felt calmer when I was there. Once I was able to relax my muscles and body, the next step was to learn to focus on a candle. When I did that, I wasn't distracted by thoughts of what had happened in my life. I wasn't thinking about what was going to happen. I was just sitting there relaxed. She taught me how to just be.

By the end of that six-week period, I had no more anger, no more hostility and no judgement of my situation. My emotional state was no longer dictating my interactions with other people, or my experience of the world. What she taught me fundamentally changed the trajectory of my life.

We've all got our protective mechanisms. For so many years, shutting myself off was my way of coping with my childhood and what I was seeing around me. Eventually, I realised that's what was happening with my father and mother, too.

Though my father was an alcoholic, he could also be an extraordinarily kind person. He was just very harsh with himself, and he hid the pain he suffered with his drinking so he wouldn't have to face it. He was really never violent in general, but the night before I was about to leave for college, he came home drunk. My mother had locked the door. He wanted in. She wouldn't open the door because she was afraid, so he kicked it in. I was now awake, and my brother was hiding.

My father was threatening, and when he came towards my mother I told him to stop, but he continued, and so I told him if he didn't stop I would hit him. He didn't stop, so I hit him on the nose and broke it. He fell to the ground, bleeding profusely. He passed out and, when he woke up, he looked at me in a different way. It was interesting ... he looked at me and said, 'It's okay.'

As I saw him there, just a frail, fragile, vulnerable human being, it gave me a sense of the depth of the pain he was suffering. I couldn't be angry. Suddenly my father, the alcoholic, all those ways I had defined him, those labels disappeared, and I really saw him for the first time. As he was.

After the experience that I had with Ruth, I didn't have the degree of anger and hostility I had previously had, but I hadn't been able to see through his eyes, and those are different things. Our relationship had been slowly evolving from one of constant altercation and hostility to just one of acceptance and love, but that certainly was a pivotal point.

It made me realise what was possible when you're not just drowning in your own pain. Understanding that so many other people were suffering, like my father and mother, allowed me to open up and to connect with them, simply to be with them, as best I could at that time. Once I was able to see them without the colours I had painted them with, and to see them as individuals with their own difficulties, their own struggles, anger and hostility was gone. It changed everything.

After I stopped his bleeding, I went to the bathroom and threw up.

Later, while I was in college, I got a call to say my father was in jail. I didn't have a car, so I had to tell a friend the situation, which was hard. He gave me a ride to the jail. I paid the bail to release my father, went up and got his possessions—which were in one suitcase—and paid for a hotel for him with all the money I had.

It was hard to see him like that, but a few weeks later, I got a letter from him. He seldom, if ever, wrote letters, and in it, he signed a cheque he'd received over to me to pay me back. And the letter said, 'I love you, Dad.'

AMANDINE | So, I believe in destiny

AMANDINE ROCHE, HUMAN RIGHTS EXPERT

We lived outside of Paris, close to the cathedral of Chartres, until I was 12 years old. It's like a suburb of Paris, very cosmopolitan, and there were a lot of migrants from Turkey, Morocco and Algeria, and other places. Living there really helped me to open my mind to different cultures. Then we moved to Bordeaux, which was very conservative and quite aristocratic. It was a big contrast.

My dad was a computer engineer and my mom was a housewife and an artist. My dad loved travelling. He bought an RV and, every holiday, all three of us kids would jump in and he would ask us where in the world we wanted to go. We went to Poland. We went to Italy many times, to Spain, Portugal, Morocco and Greece. It planted the seed for travel and curiosity about other cultures, other traditions, other people—it's in my DNA. My sister is the same. My brother, too. We have the bug. I realised I don't even know how to stop travelling and being curious.

Every year, my mom bought the UNICEF calendar. Each month featured the face of a new kid: African, Asian, South American. I would think about the life these kids had, what type of environments they lived in, and what type of education or culture they had. It put me in another world of imagination completely. That, and travelling with my parents in an RV dreaming about discovering new countries, paved the foundation of my future life.

My mom was a political refugee from Poland who fled communism. She's kind of a human rights activist. She used to take me to all these Amnesty International gatherings. One day, she took me to a place where there was a photo exhibition of torture. I was so shocked and traumatised by these pictures. I heard a voice within me say, *You're going to work on that.*

When I was a small girl, I saw into my own past lives. I remember one time before Mother's Day, my teacher said, 'Every day, do a good action for your mom.' We had a garden and there were big stones on the path between the house and the garden, so I decided to clean each of the stones. I was seven years old. I took a small bucket and a sponge and, every time I cleaned one big stone, I saw the face of a woman emerge. It was a woman on a slave boat, and she was suffering. Another woman was a prostitute or sexual slave in a harem in the Middle East. Another one, a leper in India. I saw all of these women who were poor and suffering and I asked myself, *What is this?* And I heard it was me.

I started to freak out. I said to myself, *I don't want to be a woman. I don't want to be a woman in this life. I don't want this kind of life. Why am I a woman?* I became jealous of my brother because he had a penis and I didn't have one. I started to be super pissed off with God and my parents, asking 'Why am I a woman?' At some point, when my chest started to grow, I said, *Oh no, no, no, I don't want that. I'm not going to be a woman.* It was very clear to me: my purpose had to be to release women from conditions of suffering.

My grandmother from my dad's side had a big influence on me. She was renting a house in the south of France and I would visit her every summer.

Thanks to her, my cousins and I were all scouts. We learned the skills to live and survive in nature. Definitely, she planted that seed in me to serve through humanitarian work. She was a sort of feminist and was always telling me, 'I want you to have the grace of a woman, but the strength of a man. And I want you to contribute to the world and serve humankind.' She was a big fan of Mother Teresa. She would always tell stories of people saving the world, like missionaries: you go to a country in Africa for a while, and you serve. It was very natural in my family to think that way.

I feel I would not have been normal if I *hadn't* done that, actually. All my cousins did it, too. It's just the way she educated us. When you are privileged, you give back. You are born to contribute to a better world.

My other grandmother from my Polish side, my mother's side, gave us a sense of mysticism. She taught us how to connect with the invisible, how to develop our telepathy, and that what the world needs is more love. She had a big heart, she was very generous. My grandmothers gave me these values in life.

In 1993, when I was 18 and studying human rights at university, the Dalai Lama came to give a speech. I sat in the middle of all the Tibetan monks and one of the organisers of the event said, 'You should not sit here, it's not your seat.' One of the monks double-checked my ticket, and I was in the correct seat. He said, 'No, no, no, she has to stay here.' So, when the Dalai Lama came into the room and saw the blonde girl in the middle of all the monks, he started laughing, you know, like, 'Ho, ho, ho, ho,' how the Dalai Lama laughs.

I realised by doing so, he was making me even more aware of the speech. I can repeat everything he talked about. He spoke graphically about the violation of human rights in Tibet, horrible rapes by the Chinese, and how the Tibetans were resisting all of it nonviolently.

He showed me my path—what I wanted to embrace in life: to become a human rights lawyer and join the United Nations (UN). It was very clear to me. It opened the door to express where I stood on human rights.

I did my political science thesis on the violation of human rights in Tibet. I did a Masters degree in international relations and I joined the UN at the age of 24. It was like a highway in the sense that I knew where my path lay: I followed my heart.

In 1998, my boyfriend at the time suggested we watch a documentary about Commander Massoud that was screening in Paris. He was so much in love with Commander Massoud and said, 'Oh, let's go to see the documentary.' I said, 'Oh my gosh, whoa, Afghanistan—not for me.' And I never watched it.

It's incredible how quickly things can change. One year later, I was in Tajikistan in the office of Commander Massoud. I thought, *Shit! I should have watched the documentary.* It's all destiny. I got it afterwards.

Commander Massoud was fighting against the Taliban. I met him, he gave me a visa and invited me to go by helicopter to his home in Afghanistan, but my boss didn't want me to go. I was so angry; I should have said fuck it and gone. It was my holidays, but he said, 'You can't go on your holiday because it's too dangerous.' He felt responsible for my safety. It turned out I missed a big opportunity because, shortly after that, Commander Massoud was assassinated so I never met him again. So yeah, I believe in destiny, and Afghanistan was the perfect playground for me.

'Everything is a miracle

if you want it to be. Anything.

When you get jaded, you lose

curiosity, and then you age.

But if you're curious,

there are always new beginnings.'

RABBI RONNIE CAHANA

TWO

CONDITIONED INTO A WIN-LOSE SYSTEM

Our 'operating system' is the driver of the choices we make in life, and is shaping our reality. But what if the code has a bug? What if that operating system is flawed?

Tom

When I was in high school I wanted to become a journalist and write articles for *Time* magazine, saving the world from capitalistic greed. Before I knuckled down to my degree, I took a year off to travel around the world and explore beyond the horizons of my life on a farm and at an all-boy Catholic school. I climbed mountains, travelled across

Europe on trains, roamed cobblestone streets and sat in cafes reading books by French existentialists. I felt free.

After almost of a year of this exotic, dreamy adventure, I arrived home and had a few months to fill before a life of cheap wine and two-minute noodles at university, so I applied to a bunch of jobs in the paper to save some pocket money.

One of them was at an English brokerage company my sister worked at that had set up a branch in Australia. I had seen glimpses into her life as a broker and it looked glamorous and exciting. I was offered the job on the bonds desk and, although I had every intention of leaving after four months to start my degree, it wasn't long before I knew deep down that wasn't going to happen. In a short time, they had given me a sports car, a corporate Amex card to entertain clients, and a pay rise. I was 19 years old. The job consisted of winning trades from other brokers in competing companies. The trades that I won were by bankers who were buying or selling from all around the world. When you win a trade, it's adrenaline and high-fives all round. You then go to the bar with your corporate card and continue with the celebrations. When you lose, you feel a deep sense of failure, you feel judged by your colleagues, you let the team down, then you go to the bar and drown your sorrows in expensive beer and vodka.

In the end, I spent 26 years of my life working on that same trading room floor. The same thing every day, year after year. Same seat, same clients, same phone, same markets: Groundhog Day. My dreams of saving the world were eaten up by the yearning for the next deal, the next bonus, the next dollar.

There were many profound 'aha' moments for me in the process of researching and writing this book. One of the greatest and most personally powerful was when we sat down with evolutionary philosopher Daniel Schmachtenberger and he told us about the foundation of the current global paradigm. It's easy to break down because it only has two parts: *win* and *lose*. Our world, and almost everything in it functions around a 'win-lose' relationship. This has underpinned our society for 40,000–50,000 years and is affecting nearly every aspect of our lives. The basis of the win-lose notion is fear: fear of scarce resources, the need for more, fear that others are a threat to our sustainability. Competitive advantage drives everything, and, when you extrapolate that mindset to the development of technology, as Daniel points out, the consequences on an existential level are unthinkable.

The idea that this one simple dynamic influences the entire human civilisation might seem obvious, but it dramatically opened up my understanding of the interwoven dynamics of the world, from competition for scarce resources to countries fighting for oil and political parties polling over electorates, stock markets competing for investors' money, athletics teams battling for medals—even children vying for their parents' attention. Everywhere you look, there are two (or more) people or groups (tribes) competing for scarce resources, vying to win—but someone always loses.

We get swept into the system from the day we are born, and most of us unwittingly float along with it, but the direct and indirect effects on each of us as individuals can be devastating. Whether it's direct exposure to violence; feeling pressure or seeking validation in high-level, rivalrous environments; or the urge to win, be the best and have the most (at the expense of our humanity and core values), the resulting stress is ravaging our mental health.

I considered the effects that very system had had on me over many years: I had replaced my core values with 'How can I get more?' My deeper nature to care for others and dream of a better world had been replaced by the overriding, all-consuming drive to win. My mother and father were the kindest and most generous people, always going out of their way to make society a better place. Early in my childhood, they played a big role in instilling in me the intention to help the world be better. Yet, how quickly and easily I had been pulled into the vortex of a competitive, dog-eat-dog industry. It had affected my mental health and who I was as a person—and, to this day, I carry some of those scars.

Jacqui

In a powerful blog about her time at Harvard, Due Quach wrote, 'College is a time of self-discovery, but it is particularly hard to find who you are when you attend one of the most intensely competitive, hyper-critical and hypocritical universities on the planet.'[3] She wanted to go public about the long-term damage of an environment like Harvard on students, which led many to breaking point just so they could 'make it'. Her post went viral, and that is how our team first came across her.

One of the things that Due missed during her high-pressure college years was a sense of community: small acts like people looking out for each other or noticing if a person is not okay. Generosity of spirit without motive. When she and I spent a day together driving around her old neighbourhood, I began to see that, in spite of being a complicated and often violent urban ecosystem (as she described it), there was a demonstrated spirit of caring in the community.

Due told me stories about her dad and the pride he takes in being an active part of the community. At the time of writing this book, he was the only Asian-American on the Democratic Ward Committee in their neighbourhood. He now runs a laundromat and we drove past it. The front was all boarded up and it appeared to be closed, but it wasn't. Due explained to me that if the store is closed, the neighbours won't have anywhere to wash their clothes, so he tries to keep it open, even though it can actually lose money. It was heartening to see this sign of community solidarity in our increasingly disconnected, anonymous modern society.

In this book, Due explores her past, including her personal cultural context and the experiences that shaped her. She talks about the turning points in her life that catapulted her towards different career choices. But Due is also one of several people we spoke to over the course of this project whose present-day work is directly connected to the redesign of our global human systems. She's now working with institutions and corporations to create educational and mentorship opportunities that support students, foster passion-driven project initiatives and facilitate work placements, so that first-generation college students and students from minority or disadvantaged backgrounds don't experience the same lack of support and opportunity that she and others did. Her knowledge of the system and its shortcomings has helped her find ways to subvert and reinvent it.

In many ways, Due's story is a sign of a changing tide, a testament to the reality and viability of making a personal passion your life's work, and to our collective spirit of innovation as we embark on a different model for our future.

Another of our interviewees, Heather Hennessy, came to us through 40 years of Zen, a high-tech brain-training program that uses advanced neurofeedback technology to measure and improve what's happening in our heads. Neurofeedback is a development in brain optimisation that is becoming increasingly recognised for the capacity it has to undo changes to the brain caused by trauma, and bring about greater mind-body harmony, focus and creativity. It works by measuring the electricity in the brain, turning it into sounds that can be played back to you, so that your brain gets new information (feedback) about how it's doing. It's one of the ways the principles of meditation are inspiring cutting-edge uses of technology, as this process is essentially what meditation does, but with a measurement component (feedback) that amplifies and speeds up the improvement rate. The facility Heather attended was set up by author and number-one health podcaster Dave Asprey, a 'biohacker' and founder of the Bulletproof Executive blog, which is aimed at helping its audience achieve high performance by upgrading their minds, bodies and lifestyles.

One of the things I appreciated about Heather, right from the start, was her trust in life. She persistently takes an open, committed attitude to everything she does. She's all in. Trust is a welcome quality in this fear-driven world, and it transcends a win-lose mindset because the starting point is the assumption that you're *not* going to be taken advantage of. Here is a woman who, through her meditation practice and the decisions she makes, consistently demonstrates a level of trust in the universe that says: I'm going to be okay.

To me, Heather represents the pulse of life: she's that constant forward motion. A friend once said to me that at some point you stop running away from whatever you're running from, and you start running towards yourself. I mentioned this to Heather during our interview. She got it. She's spent her whole life running, always moving forwards physically, but with a heavy emotional drag. Now, even when it's difficult, she is finding peace and joy in the forward movement because it's towards a truer expression of who she is.

the outer view

The macro effect of micro thinking

DANIEL SCHMACHTENBERGER, EVOLUTIONARY
PHILOSOPHER AND GLOBAL SYSTEMS STRATEGIST

It is not obvious at first, but everyone actually has the same values, only they weight their values very differently based on their personal 'fundamental theory of trade-offs'.

For example, if I live in a world where the only way to get electricity uses coal energy that I *know* involves harming the environment and harming ecosystems, but I can't function well in society without using that energy, then I have to rationalise doing it and reduce my empathy. That means that physical infrastructure—i.e. my house—is affecting my worldview.

If someone believes there is no way to support the economy and the environment simultaneously, then they'll either focus on the environment—at the cost of some kind of scarcity or austerity measure for the people—or say, 'Hey, we really need to boost the economy, we're going to have to sacrifice the environment.'

Economics is the meeting point between our values systems and what we actually give power to and what we build. It is a tangible value system. You can actually think about economics as a kind of collective intelligence that is affecting and conditioning all the humans within the system. However, it doesn't depend on any of the people in particular.

To give you an example of this system, a whale in the ocean has huge value to how oceans work. Its extrinsic value is that it's helping the coral, it's helping the whole ecosystem by causing trophic cascades that allow the ocean to actually do photosynthesis. But because it's not on anyone's balance sheet, the economic value of the whale is zero. However, if we kill the whale and sell the meat in a whale-meat industry, that same whale might represent a million dollars worth of value. That means that, for the fisherman, there is no advantage at all in leaving the whale alive in the ocean, but there is a million dollars worth of advantage in killing it.

This would also be true for every animal alive in an ecosystem: having no economic value but, once killed, having a commodity value. For any tree in an ecosystem, for minerals in the ground, for intactness of the environment, there is no economic value. As we take things from the balance sheet of the commons—those shared resources that belong to everyone—we are actually causing a cost *somewhere*, but somewhere that we don't measure. And so, what that means is that we actually don't value nature alive, economically, but we do value it extracted, abstracted, commodified—dead. That's why we have such extreme species extinction, biodiversity loss, environmental destruction and the obliteration of 90 per cent of the world's largest fish species, because that's actually what the economic system incentivises.

And you cannot prevent a problem that you are economically incentivising, right? If we incentivise agents of any kind—corporations, countries, people—to do things that directly or indirectly cause harm, those things will happen. Right now, the system does that everywhere. It's what is called 'perverse incentive'.

Fundamentally, when you recognise that living ecosystems are not incentivised in that system anywhere, but the conversion of those living ecosystems to commodities is, there is a finite amount of time that you can do that for before the system self-terminates.

To understand the value of a natural resource, you have to understand its value to its beneficiaries in its exact context. To pollinators, the tree provides food, nectar, pollen, and so on. To the soil, it provides micro-organisms that have a symbiotic relationship with the tree's roots. For the fish in the river, the tree stabilises the topsoil from rain and keeps the river clean. Where the river dumps into the ocean onto a coral reef, that coral reef is affected by the tree that is stabilising the topsoil. And of course the people who are eating the fish are healthier as a result of the fish swimming in cleaner water.

Now, we don't attribute any economic value to any of that, even though our lives depend on all of it. We depend on the pollinators to pollinate our crops. We depend on soil stabilisation to prevent massive floods and dead zones in the ocean. We depend on our atmosphere, which the tree helps to create—in fact, it's maintaining that atmosphere.

But what happens if I cut this one tree down? Will it affect all of those things? The answer is no, well, not directly. The problem is that if everyone—all 7.8 billion people—think this way, no one actually takes responsibility for the macro effect of that micro-thinking process. So I see the advantage in taking this one tree out of the environment and turning it into two-by-fours, but I don't notice the damage to the commons. Everyone doing that at scale eventually brings the commons to the point of criticality and failure.

What we have called civilisation so far is taking this natural-world complexity and making simple stuff out of it. Humans are taking a tree that is self-organising and adaptive to its environment and making two-by-fours that are not self-organising, self-repairing or self-healing, which is making the complex simple. That's the exact opposite direction of evolution. And you can only do that for so long before you actually lose the resilience of the system, because a system's resilience is proportional to its complexity.

Unlike the complex, self-repairing ecosystem, humans build complicated systems that cannot repair themselves. A house is not self-repairing and a computer is not self-repairing. If you damage water lines, you damage the grid, and they do not repair automatically. Humans have created a system that is fundamentally fragile. And more and more people are depending on this increasingly fragile, complicated system, while the underlying complex ecosystem is also becoming more and more fragile as the total biodiversity is removed from it.

Civilisation cannot continue this way. Once we understand that evolution naturally increases the orderly complexity of everything, we need to become agents for that and create a civilisation that is complex, not complicated, where our built world is complex, not complicated. At that point, we can begin to see the human built world as an extension of the elegant, ordered complexity of the natural world.

The primatologist Robin Dunbar came up with the famous Dunbar number.[4] This number, which is around 150, describes the size of different primate groups and how their size is related to their capacity for processing numbers of unique relationships. He looked at indigenous societies that always capped out around 150, maybe up to around 200, people. He found that any society greater than that bifurcates. Dunbar theorised that this was the result of our limited cognitive capacity to process unique and stable relationships. For example, if I've grown up with 150 people my whole life, I actually have real relationships with all of them and can track that many people in depth. This means that I can't hurt any of those people without hurting someone I know deeply. But as soon as a society reaches the number of people where some of them become anonymous (over 150–200), and I don't know them that well, I don't notice it or feel it when harm is happening to them, and I could potentially perpetrate some kind of direct or indirect harm because I have lost my sense of connection and empathy towards those people.

When we look at the time before agriculture in human history, we can see that when resources were abundant in an area, the people in that area were mostly peaceful. This is oversimplified, but important. When the population increased relative to scarce resources in an area, scarcity-driven tensions arose, as tribes competed for those scarce resources. That tension manifested in competition to see who could extract the scarce resources from the environment faster and, if needed, engage in actual military competition.

Then, not only do the groups get larger, but their capacity to compete for scarce-resource extraction increases. They go from using axes to cut down trees, to using chainsaws to slash and burn whole ecosystems. So they're increasing their capacity to extract resources and, at the same time, increasing military and propaganda capacity to keep people on their side and not defect to other sides. So when we look at the evolutionary curve, we can see that humans have been increasing their technological capacity the whole time, but not on a linear curve—on an exponential curve.

As soon as a tribe commenced military action—attacking other tribes to keep them from competing for scarce resources, or to acquire those resources they had already obtained—then all the other tribes had to engage or lose by default. As soon as anybody plays the militaristic game, everybody has to play or you just lose.

If we look at any of the major environmental issues we're facing today—biodiversity loss, climate change or species extinction—or any of the other human-induced catastrophes, such as war, economic collapse or wrongly applied exponential technology, they all have the same underlying generator function: win-lose games multiplied by exponential power. And we've always been motivated by win-lose games. It doesn't mean there aren't pockets that didn't do otherwise, but those pockets usually lost in a win-lose kind of Darwinian fashion, usually militaristically. So we can see that the existential risks are actually a result of underlying system dynamics, which you can't actually isolate.

Direct and indirect harm from win-lose games has always been a part of the system, but in the past we had limited power. When you go from stone weapons to spears, to guns, to intercontinental ballistic missiles, you can't keep doing the same thing, because the playing field can't handle the dynamics of that much power. So when we reflect on the current global scenario we're faced with, where the outcomes of decisions we make carry so much power, we are forced to make better decisions or self-terminate.

the inner view: part 2

BOODA | In war, nobody wins

RON 'BOODA' TAYLOR, RETIRED US ARMY SERGEANT

In the military, you have to work as a cohesive unit. That was a culture shock for me. My first battle buddy was from Oregon and he had never seen a black man before. All he knew was that black guys were usually gangsters and were violent. It just so happened that I was a gangster and violent. He was afraid of me. On my side, I'd never been friends with a white guy. It was weird. We were forced to have each other's backs. We were the odd couple. I don't hold on to relationships all that well, but he and I became best friends.

I was sent to Pensacola, Florida, where I learned to be a combat photographer, but at first it was mainly darkroom stuff I was doing, and ceremonies. I then went overseas, to Japan, to work as a studio photographer initially. We were then tasked with assisting criminal investigations throughout the country and documenting bilateral training exercises with our Japanese counterparts. Once I left Japan I went to the National Training Center at Fort Irwin in California where I was an observer controller, or OC. The National Training Center is basically the step before going into active combat. My role there was to document the battlefield, and how units would act and react in situations that they would likely encounter. I did that for almost two years. Leaving there, I went to Hawaii where I was part of a Joint POW/MIA Accounting Command, where we would go to countries in Southeast Asia and recover the remains of soldiers from various wars, mainly Vietnam.

Once, I had to document an airman who had committed suicide. He jumped from the ninth story of an apartment building on the base. I had to document his body, his remains—the whole scene. I had to go through the actual investigation piece with investigators, read the suicide note, and go over the forensics with the computer. I actually knew this guy, so it was really tough. I thought, *What would drive a man to do that?* He had a wife and two kids; one of them was a newborn.

Leaving there, I changed my job to Military Intelligence and started the second phase of my military career. I chose geospatial intel', which was work with the drone guys. We were the eyes for the drones. It's what I did in Afghanistan. We analysed everything in the middle of combat. It's quick. Did you see it? Yes or no? The minute you say yes, you've got the launch. Then it's sitting watching a hit take place on high-definition TV. No judge, no jury. You said yes, so all these people have to die. They get blown to pieces. And you watch it all.

A mission came up that I loved the name of, so I thought, *Yeah, this is mine. I want to do this one.* I was in charge of the whole thing. I had my soldiers who actually worked the mission while I just supervised it, and we were getting ready to strike.

To be honest, I was never a fan of it. I understood that it was a necessary part of being on a mission, and that if I didn't do my part, it didn't just affect me—it affected the guys on the ground and the overall mission. At the end of the day, I was there to save and protect my people, so I did.

Ramping up a strike automatically draws attention to everybody in the control centre because it's live on a big screen. All the senior guys come and want to see what's going on, and we have to get authorisation from every level. So I'm sitting there on this mission and I literally have the Colonel over my shoulder and he's like, 'What do you see?' And I told him. I pointed it out. He said okay and authorised it, so I communicate that with my guys, and boom! The mission's over.

We'd hunt humans, watching and waiting for the right opportunity to strike. It plays on your mind. Other times, we'd fly over looking for IEDs (improvised explosive devices), mines, et cetera. Sometimes I missed them and soldiers got killed. I literally watched it happen. But this isn't a video game, it's real. *What I just did was real.* How would I feel if that was my family, somebody I loved or cared about? I personalised it.

There are things that happen in war that you have no control over. It's war and that's the unfortunate thing about it—nobody wins. I kill you and you kill me. I kill more of you and you kill more of me and it just goes on and on until one side gets tired of dying. You're just beaten into submission, but who wins, really? Does that mean we become friends now that it's over? It doesn't. It never actually ends.

When service members return home, they go from one extreme environment to another. Being deployed in any capacity, you're always ready to go. It's an instinct after so much specialised training—at least a year's worth, if not more, of preparing to go into that particular environment. You just react. React, react, react. You don't really think about the toll it's going to take on you mentally. But, at home, it's in those quiet moments at night when I'm not able to sleep that I replay everything in my head.

I'm constantly looking around, constantly analysing the situation. I can never calm down. I have motion detectors in the house so I can see if somebody is walking around. And with all that security, I can't sleep. I still think something's wrong. I still sit up at night. I can't relax. I'm always looking for something to go wrong and I want to be ready.

What never goes away is the smell, the sound, the visions of seeing bodies and then knowing that I played a role. A big role. I'm sad that I had to do that, but, on the flip side, I also saw what happened when we were too slow to react and US soldiers got killed. Someone has to call the loved ones and tell them their son or daughter is not coming back because you didn't do your job. It plays in your head. *It's my fault. Is it really my fault? I don't know. I feel like it is. I was too slow. I was too hesitant. I didn't want to make that call. I wasn't sure.*

War makes you see the worst in man. You see how bad we are. How destructive we can be. The world's a beautiful place and there are a lot of kind, beautiful people in it, but there are also a lot of horrible and heartless people. And seeing that does something to you. I didn't grow up in the best environment, but war makes that look like day care.

DUE | My ticket to freedom

DUE QUACH, SOCIAL ENTREPRENEUR AND REFUGEE

So you get to Harvard and all your dreams come true, right? I felt like my nightmares came true. I think I was just really naïve about what I was getting myself into. For me, it felt like making it to Harvard was my prize for the years of working my butt off for my parents and doing good in school. But when I got there, it was just a lot more work and a lot more pressure. My family offered no emotional support either; everyone back home thought I had it easy. They didn't understand the pressure and challenges of being a first-generation college student. Being forced to navigate between such extreme ends of the socioeconomic spectrum alone, at such a young age, drove me to the verge of insanity.

I didn't understand until I got to Harvard that what I had experienced in childhood was not normal. At Harvard, I was surrounded by people who had such high expectations and were so perfection-oriented and neurotic. Most of my classmates lived very privileged and sheltered lives, and those with whom I shared my story were horrified. Harvard was this ivory tower bubble, where people lived in a way that just didn't make sense to me. And the amount of pressure they put on themselves and each other, and the level of criticism, and the level of expectation, I thought was just not sustainable. It didn't surprise me to learn that many of the people I met were actually depressed, had anxiety or needed counselling and therapy. It was very normal at Harvard to have a therapist.

When I was a freshman, my grandmother passed away. I didn't have a strong social support network at Harvard, and I didn't know how to process the grief. On the one hand she was my grandmother, and we took care of her for as long as I could remember. But she was suffering and became a vegetable the last few years of her life. I was relieved that we no longer had that burden, but I felt guilty for feeling relieved. I didn't understand how to process those emotions. I was full of anger at all the sacrifices we had made to take care of her, and how violent her mental illness was, and how unfair it all seemed.

That was when these crying spells started that I couldn't stop. I started having flashbacks and disassociation. I couldn't focus in class. I could barely write. I could barely do my problem sets. At first, I just thought it was grief and would pass. But it didn't.

By that point, I was an art major, and I found making art to be very therapeutic, so that helped calm the symptoms for a while. But the crying spells continued. When I tried to sleep, I had horrible nightmares. And whatever reel was playing out in my head, it was pretty catastrophic. I just couldn't stop it. I felt a total lack of control over what was happening.

I used to go for walks and try to breathe, but all the time I'd be thinking, *That's a nice roof to jump off.* These ideas would come up, and I had to tell myself, *Just stay away from that roof.* There was this voice in my head that was very hopeless and self-destructive, and it was just saying, *This isn't worth it anymore. It's pointless.* A number of suicides happened while I was at Harvard, and it became obvious that I wasn't the only person with this negative voice in their head.

I felt so toxic. It was like I was seeing the world through shit-coloured glasses. I was so angry. Then, one day, a friend said to me, 'You know, you're just not that pleasant to be around. You just complain all day. Can't you change the topic or talk about something positive?' That made me question why I couldn't see the positive. *Why did I only see the negative?* It became clearer that maybe there was something wrong with my brain, and that maybe *I* was the problem. Maybe it wasn't that the world had to change, but that I had to take off these shit-coloured glasses.

When I finally decided to get help, it was my senior year. I was having too many panic attacks. I'd even taken myself to the emergency room because I couldn't breathe. They gave me Ativan and that calmed me down. Since it worked, I decided to try medication. I went to see a psychiatrist and he said, 'Walk me through your life story.'

After I told the psychiatrist my story, he said, 'You went through a lot of trauma before you were two years old. We now know that these things you go through in the first two years of life affect your personality, and they affect the development of your brain.' He implied that early childhood trauma could be a life sentence, because it can affect brain development in ways that can result in lifelong challenges.

While most people have heard of post-traumatic stress disorder, or PTSD, many are unaware of how widespread childhood trauma is. The scientific term for it is adverse childhood experience, or ACE for short. About two out of three people have experienced at least one ACE. Experiencing at least four ACEs became recognised as the threshold for severe trauma, because the risk of developing serious health issues, addictions and self-destructive behaviours increased dramatically at that point. Researchers added five new indicators to include traumatic experiences common among an urban population, such as witnessing violence, experiencing racism, living in an unsafe neighbourhood, experiencing bullying and living in foster care. I had experienced four of the five new indicators.[5]

He explained that there was no guarantee of a cure, which meant it was possible I could struggle with these symptoms the rest of my life. What was the point of getting into Harvard only to have my brain turn against me?

Though I felt extremely disappointed hearing that diagnosis, I was also relieved because, finally, I learned that what I was going through didn't mean that I was a wimp, or I was weak. It meant the opposite: that I was ridiculously resilient. Even though I was disassociating and having all these issues, I still managed to get As and A minuses. I think the worst grade I ever got was a B.

I was wearing the trauma ridiculously well. I was highly functional. But suppressing the trauma had created this condition called anhedonia, which is the inability to feel pleasure anymore. I was numb. I stopped feeling good. I just couldn't have fun, I couldn't smile. I had no energy and no motivation.

I asked the psychiatrist, 'What can we do about this?' And he said, 'You know, there's not a lot of research on curing these symptoms. We know now that antidepressants often help.' He also suggested therapy. So, I said, 'Okay, fine. Give me what you got.'

So I started taking the antidepressant prescribed by the psychiatrist to alter my brain chemistry and soften the panic attacks. I also started therapy. In a few months, I felt more stable, but once my student health insurance expired, I would no longer be able to afford these treatments. Therefore, graduation from Harvard became a deadline for getting off the drugs and therapy.

Turns out, when we experience trauma over the long term, our brains, minds and lives are reorganised, as if that trauma were still going on. Our brains stay hyper-activated, and the functioning of the frontal lobes becomes impaired. We can get trapped in a chronic negative emotional state when the trauma disrupts the left prefrontal cortex. Bodily sensations that remind us of the trauma can become overwhelming. So we often adapt by disassociating to block, suppress and numb painful sensations and memories. At my worst, it was like an inner Godzilla took over me, making me want to smash things or disappear. I felt overwhelmed with fear and anxiety, and could only see what could go wrong.

This feels awful, so then we try to escape those feelings by drinking, eating, shopping or gambling to feel any type of high, that takes our minds off being miserable. This shuts down our neural circuits for self-control, the braking system that keeps us from doing horrible things and hurting our loved ones and ourselves. It is such a vicious cycle; I had no idea that's what had been going on.

Once I learned about PTSD, it didn't take me long to wonder if maybe my parents had it, too. They would relive these flashbacks of things that weren't happening, but they would act like it was happening. I realised they were often stuck in the past and they let their fears drive their behaviour.

The more I learned, the more progress I made. I began to be a lot more selective about who I spent time with. I didn't want to activate my neural circuits for negative emotions any more than they were already activated. I stopped watching depressing movies and tried to watch more comedies and read more jokes. I stopped playing negative, angry music and tried to play more uplifting music. I did everything I could to try to activate my circuitry for positive emotions, because it was under-utilised.

Everything I learned about the brain gave me more compassion for what I was going through. I learned not to personalise it as much, realising that I wasn't the only person having these issues. It's part of the human condition.

'Happiness is believing in your

life force. It *is* your life force.

We shouldn't squander it.'

RABBI RONNIE CAHANA

HEATHER | The disease to please

HEATHER HENNESSY, FORMER US NATIONAL TRACK
ATHLETE AND SPORTS TV PRESENTER

As a teenager, I felt in control of my fate. I thought I was going to find a way to make my running career happen. *I'm going to be the best and no one is going to take this away from me.* I didn't want to have a plan B. It is what made me successful but, obviously, through my accident, I learned that much of life is not within your control.

Ever since I was a young child, I trained hard and visualised how I would become the national running champion and win a spot on the US Olympic team. During my junior year at Los Gatos High School in California, when I was 17, I was fast enough to be in the national finals of the 800 metre race, competing against other state champions from across the nation.

There was a CCS (Central Coast Sectional) race that I was really set on; winning the sectionals would take me to the state meet, and my goal had always been to win the state meet. I wanted to win the state of California. That was a huge race for me.

When I ran my races, I usually tailed the person in the lead. Because I had a lot of speed, I would beat them at the end. But in this particular race, when I went to pass the girl, she kind of pushed me, and I kind of pushed her back.

I ended up winning the race.

Then this weird thing happened afterwards. The officials ended up disqualifying me, which was ridiculous considering that we had pushed each other, and that I had won the race by quite a distance. The next day, I woke up and saw my disqualification splashed across the front of the local paper. I was extremely embarrassed and upset … and my father was devastated. My parents encouraged me to keep going, so I got back up and I thought, *Okay*. My coach came to me and said, 'Let's put you in the national race. You can still enter.' That disqualification could have stopped me. I could have just given up at that point, but I said, 'Let's go to the national meet.' I just kept pushing.

I was the underdog in the race—no one expected me to be a contender. They were talking up all the other girls and the girls who had won the state meet, and I just kept thinking, *I'm going to show them*. I had done a lot of visualising for that race, seeing myself win, and the disqualification had definitely lit a fire in me.

When the race began, one of the girls (ranked number two in the country) took off really fast and, at 400 metres, she was way out ahead. My coach had told me there was a certain time in the race to make my move because even in the 800 metres, it's a sprint, but there's a lot of strategy that goes into it. You have a plan, but you have to listen to that gut feeling and go off instinct. That's the big thing with the 800.

For me, it was exactly that. Going into the last 400 metres, even though the girl was so far ahead of me, I kept thinking, *I am not losing this race. I have to go now*. Usually I would wait longer, but I just had that voice saying, *Go, go—go now, don't worry about dying at the end, just go for it*. So I thought, *Screw it*. The last 400 metres, I just went for it.

I reached her at about the last 200 metres. I gave it everything I had and I kept thinking positive affirmations, like: *I am doing this. I am winning this. I am not letting anyone or anything stop me*. Everything that had been building up in me throughout my entire childhood—all of the abuse at the hands of my father—I just took it all out in that race. It was my key to freedom.

It all came together in that moment. Everything just clicked and it felt like I was achieving what I had always dreamed of. I became number one in the nation in that race.

When you work so hard and you have a dream and you see it unfold—there's no feeling like that. I proved everyone wrong who doubted me, and I think that actually showed more about my character and my determination.

College recruiters immediately began calling me. I had offers for track scholarships to Stanford University, Harvard University, Duke, UCLA and USC (the University of Southern California) in Los Angeles. It was what I had been dreaming of and visualising for so many years and it was all happening.

A couple of weeks later, everything changed in a split second: I broke my back. I went from a feeling of total euphoria to thinking *I could die, or I could be paralysed.*

We were on a trip to Lake Tahoe with our coaches when it happened. We had gathered at a cliff overlooking a river. It was a team tradition to jump from this high ledge into the water. One by one, we took turns jumping off the 60 foot cliff. When it was my turn, I stood looking over the edge. I got very tense. My intuition was screaming, *Don't do this!* I didn't want to jump. But I didn't listen.

That's the thing about peer pressure, especially at that age. I never usually caved to peer pressure—I wasn't a partier. I wasn't a drinker. I really did pride myself on taking care of my body because I had such big goals. But this time, it felt different because I was with my track team. I was the team captain and I was keen to participate in this bonding experience. My coach had been like a second father to me, and my team felt like my family. I didn't want to let them down.

The drop off the cliff was 60 feet, high up over water, and they were all encouraging me: 'Come on, it's fine. Just jump.'

I closed my eyes and held my breath, and just sort of flew myself out over the cliff without really knowing what I was doing. As I got into the air, I realised how powerful a jump it was. I immediately lost control and thought, *This wasn't a good idea.* It all happened so quickly. I had this feeling like, *Oh my God, I could die. I've got to pull up.* I was afraid I would land on my head.

As I hit the water, everything in my body just crunched.

I remember the splash. I remember when I hit the surface, how it felt like concrete. I couldn't move. I couldn't breathe. The only thing I could do was to tell the coach to call 911.

Pain was shooting up throughout my body. The impact had compressed my spine, shattered my pelvis, and broken my back. It was the first time that I disconnected fully from my body. I couldn't feel it at all, it was like this out-of-body experience. The paramedics put me on a stretcher and carried me up a trail, and the ride to the hospital in the ambulance was terrible, so extremely excruciating.

That trip, that moment, was the major turning point for me. My whole life, I've had really good intuition. I had won that race because of that 'feeling'—because I trusted it. Then here I was ignoring that intuitive voice. I didn't listen to my body. And I spent a lot of years regretting that.

The day after the accident, I woke up in hospital and just felt pain. Everywhere. It started to really hit me, the impact of it. The pain. The headaches. But it also felt like a dream in a way. It was so strange to go from what my life had just been, running and winning, to being unable to move.

It was hard enough being in severe pain, but equally difficult was trying to process what this accident meant for my future. It wasn't just about winning a race for me, or just going to college. For me, my running career was really a way out. I didn't have the money to pay for a college like USC. I didn't get any free handouts growing up. What would happen to my scholarships and to my future? How would I cope with this?

It was a dark period of my life. For weeks afterwards, as I was lying on a mattress at home with my mom, I went through this grieving process of being angry and depressed. I felt mad at myself for jumping. I felt mad at my coach for letting it happen. I was mad at God for giving me this gift, then taking it away.

There was a lot of confusion and a lot of sadness. Would I ever recover and be able to run and compete again? Would I even be able to walk? I went from being in the best shape of my life to, all of a sudden, hardly being able to use my body.

It's in those moments when you ask yourself, *Why does life have these really tough struggles? Why does it have to be* so *hard?* I wasn't just scared of losing my career; I was scared that I would never be normal again.

JIM | We let others destroy our dreams

JAMES R. DOTY MD, NEUROSURGEON AND NEUROSCIENTIST

Ruth was the one who told me about the voices in my head. I had created a story in there—I didn't even realise I was doing it—and it was very, very negative. *I don't deserve love, I'm not good enough. My life and dysfunctional family circumstances are my fault. I deserve to be in the situation I'm in, so why would I expect anything different?* She made me understand that was a construct and not real. It was just something I *thought* was real.

Thinking about myself with so much negativity had caused me a lot of pain. And, without meaning to, I had put a wedge between myself and other people. That began to change once I started to recognise when it was happening, and to learn a way to change the dialogue from negative to positive, making me feel like I deserved to be loved. I deserved kindness. I deserved to be embraced. That the parts of me that I thought were defective or weren't good enough didn't even exist. Using self-affirmations taught me self-compassion.

What I also didn't realise at that time was that, as human beings, we have incredible powers of interpretation—of facial expressions, body language, even smells—and we make judgements about those. When I responded to the narrative that I had attached to events, it made me angry. It made me fearful. It made me anxious. That anger, that hostility, that fear, the anxiousness then dictated how I interacted with others. When I was able to rewrite that narrative of how people saw me, the world changed for me in an extraordinary way.

One of the things that I found, once I was able to stop focusing on what I *didn't* have, when the voices in my head weren't telling me that *I couldn't possibly do that*, and I felt I had the freedom and capability to do anything, was that my curiosity naturally and dramatically increased. It's something that I've noticed in many ways over the course of my life. I stopped being afraid to reach out to other people to ask questions. I felt more creative. I started designing things like furniture, and my house. I allowed my mind to dream about how I would like things to be and how to create them.

When I was in private practice as a neurosurgeon in Southern California, one of the things I became involved with was a technology that a friend of mine had developed. He had started a company and I was so excited about it that I said I wanted to invest in it. And to trial the prototype in my practice.

It was an extraordinary innovation called CyberKnife, which was developed to treat tumours in the body with incredible accuracy. Prior to this device, the treatment of certain types of tumours required 40–60 sessions of radiation. What this technology allowed you to do was to potentially limit that to one simple treatment. While you were on the treatment table, it would take an image of your skull or your skeleton—or of what we call 'fiducials' that had been implanted—and, from that, triangulate where you were in three-dimensional space. A robot with a miniaturised radiation-therapy device could then aim the radiation through multiple entry points and treat the tumour with incredible accuracy, pinpointing the exact location without needing to spread radiation to other parts of the body. This change was profound.

The problem was that after they developed the technology, they were unable to get FDA approval and they ran out of money. So, I decided to help save the company. Many people thought I was crazy because, at the time, I didn't have any significant entrepreneurial experience. But I was also certain that the company was going to fail and that they had something unique and life-changing to offer the medical community.

I ended up at a bar having a drink and thinking about this, and began talking to a fellow next to me, who, as it turned out, was involved in finance. I convinced him to dedicate his time and effort to helping me save this company, and we ended up raising about $30 million in different types of investment and financing. Because I'd had such success in the financing of it, those involved wanted me to take up the role of CEO. So I walked away from my private practice and took the job. We were able to obtain FDA approval fairly rapidly and, ultimately, the company went public for $1.3 billion. More importantly, that device has since saved thousands of lives throughout the world.

Over the years, a lot of my success has been due to my decisiveness about what it was I wanted to achieve. I didn't let the usual obstacles and negativity—mine or other people's—limit my success. I remember when I first decided I was going to be a doctor: I was in fourth grade. A paediatrician visited my class on careers day who was so open and so kind—when I asked him a question he treated me like an equal. He didn't talk down to me. He didn't make me feel embarrassed. What he told me about how much he loved being a physician made a huge impact on me.

Now, talking about becoming a doctor and actually becoming a doctor are two different things, especially for someone like me, growing up in poverty with no role models and no access. I didn't have any money. I was completely clueless as to how to become a doctor. As I got older, I was assigned a guidance counsellor, but that person had already decided that I was not going to go to college. Fortunately, because of my childhood experience being mentored by Ruth, I no longer believed that certain things were out of bounds for me.

I did eventually get accepted into college, but the combination of having to work to support myself and trying to be successful academically was too much, and it affected my grades. When it came time to apply to medical school, my grade-point average (GPA) was 2.53—the average GPA of successful applicants to medical school was 3.79.

To think that you could go to medical school with that type of GPA, in many people's minds, was laughable. I had many friends who laughed and told me that I wasn't ever going to be able to achieve that dream. I wasn't going to let that stop me though.

At the time, you had to go to a pre-med committee to get a letter of recommendation for medical school. I went to the office and asked the secretary for my appointment to get my letter of recommendation. She looked at my file and told me that she wasn't going to give me an appointment.

I asked why not.

She looked up and said, 'Because it's a waste of everyone's time.'

I looked her in the eye and said, 'I appreciate what you're saying, but I'm not leaving here until you give me an appointment. If you want to call security, that's fine, but I'm not leaving.' Reluctantly, she gave me an appointment.

I showed up for my appointment and I remember it very clearly. I walked into a room and there were three people sitting there. Their body language was dismissive and the person in the centre—the most senior person—picked up my file and threw it on the table. He said, 'Okay, you have your appointment. Say what you have to say so that we can be done with this.'

I looked at him and said, 'Who gave you the right to destroy people's dreams? You have made judgements about me and you don't even know me. All you know is something written on a piece of paper about a GPA, and that GPA isn't me. You don't know anything about my struggles, my successes, who I am, or even my potential in any way, and you insult me because you won't even consider doing that. That's not acceptable.'

It's so easy to look at people in power and feel powerless. To shrink away, and not even try to face them. But I believed in who I was and my intention, and I spent the next 45 minutes telling them there's not one shred of evidence beyond an above-average level of intelligence that you can succeed in anything, and there's no correlation between a GPA and success in life. At the end of it, they were all crying. I wasn't going to let them essentially objectify me as a number. I forced them to look at my humanity.

I ended up getting the highest letter of recommendation you could get. As I walked out of that meeting, the secretary had a smile on her face. She had been listening in. She handed me this green brochure that was mimeographed for a summer program at Tulane University in New Orleans, for those who were pre-med and who were from lower socioeconomic backgrounds. She said, 'I want to give you this brochure because I think the program would be great for you.' Then she smiled again and said, 'The deadline has passed, but I don't think that will be an issue for you.'

When we think that our worth or identity is in the hands of someone else, we're giving our power away and giving away who we are.

Later, I called the woman from the summer program at Tulane University. She let me in. Afterwards, I got accepted into medical school with a 2.53 GPA.

AMANDINE | Haunting me like a ghost

AMANDINE ROCHE, HUMAN RIGHTS EXPERT

When I joined the UN, I worked on peacekeeping operations: democratisation and human rights. I was working on the elections, explaining to the population what 'human rights' and 'democracy' meant; what is a 'parliament', what is a 'constitution' and why you should vote for a new president. It was a fascinating time to be in Afghanistan, because it was after the Taliban regime and it was a new El Dorado. Everything had to be rebuilt. At that time, Afghanistan attracted *la crème de la crème* in a sense: the best politicians, the best diplomats, the best photographers, journalists and humanitarians from all around the world. They came with an ideal, actually, to help bring more peace, democracy, health and education to this country. It was good for the mind. It really nurtured my soul at this time.

We hired and trained a team of civic educators—teachers, engineers, doctors and so on. They were going everywhere: into mosques, into hospitals, into schools and into bazaar markets. My female colleagues were even doing door-to-door campaigns just to say to the women, 'Get out. It's a free country now. You can express yourself. You can become a leader. You can be a senator. Go and vote.'

I did this type of job with the UN for almost 20 years, working on 20 peace processes around the world. What I really liked about it was that you contribute to the elevation of consciousness in the community. You point a light on something.

I have so much respect and love and compassion for the Afghans; they are some of the most incredible people I have ever met in my life.

They're so hospitable and kind, even when the environment they're living in is pretty rough and tough, and really not an easy place to live. Literally every day there are bombings, assassinations and death threats. That's daily life.

One night in 2012, I had arrived back in Kabul from Burma. I was super jet-lagged as I had flown from Bangkok to Islamabad, Islamabad to Kabul, or I don't know what, something like that, or Delhi, Delhi to Kabul. I took some melatonin to help me sleep and slept very deeply. At 4 am there was a bombing above my roof. I jumped up in bed and opened the window. I just couldn't believe my eyes—there was a rocket flying above my roof. I was not aware that when you launch a rocket there is a flame in the back, and I literally felt like I received the flame of the rocket coming through my window. Welcome back to Afghanistan.

All night on Facebook, I was checking to see where the attacks were coming from. We were in the triangle. It was the parliament, Darul Aman and Shahr-e Naw: three areas of Kabul, and my house was in the middle, which was completely crazy.

Despite everything, Afghans are very resilient people and there are so many positive values to learn from them. That's why I love Afghanistan so much. They are very courageous, they never complain. I guess their religion really helps them. They say, 'Allah gives, Allah takes.' It's okay. It's part of life. It's pretty remarkable, really.

The Afghans speak the language of the heart, but they are mixed. In one respect, they are strong and tough like a mountain and, in the other, soft and mystical, like my two grandmothers actually.

I realised that there were many similarities between the Polish and the Afghans. They have nothing materially and they give you everything. They are authentic. They're not pretending or whatever.

It's real. After meeting them I said, 'I want to know more about these people. I feel like I have found my tribe.' And then, when I was trying to evacuate from Afghanistan in 2001 after the events of 9/11, I had a terrifying but eye-opening experience that woke up my consciousness to the fragility of the people there, especially the women and girls, and refocused my mind about the work I wanted to do.

We had come by car to the Pakistani border. (I'm talking about before the American bombing had begun.) But the border was already closed—the Pakistani government had decided to close it to stop the flow of up to 35 million Afghan refugees into Pakistan. The border guard told me that only the Taliban could give instructions to open the gate to leave Afghanistan.

Because we were among the last foreigners in the country, the Taliban guy at the customs office at the border refused to let us leave. He wanted to ransom me and my friend. While my friend was negotiating our release, I was freaking out and, to distract and calm myself, I went to play with three Afghan girls, about 10 or 11 years old. Even amid all the chaos awaiting us, they were just so happy playing. And, for a moment, my fear disappeared, too. We were singing and counting in French and Persian, laughing and having such a good time.

In a way, we got lucky. What saved us this day was one of the Taliban stepping on a landmine. He lost his leg, and the Taliban asked the Pakistanis to open the gate so he could get to a hospital close by, in Peshawar—otherwise he was going to die. The Pakistani border guard said, 'We're not going to open the gate until you release the two French people.' It was so kind of him, and the Taliban agreed to open the gate and release us.

One of the small girls I was playing with took my hand, pointed to the sky, and said, 'Peshawar, Peshawar, Peshawar.' I saw the terror in her eyes. And I understood she was scared of the American bombing and was asking me to help her get to Pakistan, so I put her in our car.

We had only one minute to cross the border because the Pakistani guard and the Taliban guard were going to open the gates at the same time. We had to drive quickly to avoid a big flow of refugees crossing the border when they did. I saw a line of refugees who were travelling by foot, by donkey, bike and truck, to flee into Pakistan. Everyone was scrambling to save their life.

Just when we were about to cross, my friend saw the girl in the back seat. 'The girl can't come,' he said. I told him she wanted to go to Pakistan with us, but he said it was impossible because she might have a family and I couldn't adopt her. I didn't want to, but I had to ask her to get out. I had to leave her; I had no choice. And I will never forget the look in her eyes.

I turned my back just to say bye to the girl, and she was in front of this huge flow of refugees. She just waved goodbye with her hand, and she cried.

Afterwards, she came back to me in my dreams every night. At 4 am I would wake up, her eyes coming towards me. And every night she looked at me and asked me the same question: 'Why didn't you save me?'

I started to become crazy, her question coming back again and again as a nightmare. My heart broke. I couldn't sleep. I asked my friend to help me, because I felt like her memory was haunting me like a ghost. He suggested writing her a letter.

So I did, and in the letter I wrote, 'My dear barefoot Afghan princess, I'm very sorry I couldn't help you. I couldn't adopt you, but I promise I will come back to help your brothers and sisters to live in a more peaceful and democratic country.'

She succeeded in her mission, because I did go back. She is the reason I returned to Afghanistan and committed myself to women's empowerment for so many years. It is all thanks to her: my small, Afghan princess, as I call her. She symbolises all the girls and women in Afghanistan who are suffering abuse and repression.

I'm all about women. The situation of women is worse, so it makes sense when I look back. There was no mistake in my past. I asked myself many times what I was doing in Afghanistan. My dad, too, would say 'What are you doing spending so many years there?' It's because I had something important to do.

'In life, everything, ultimately,

is a privilege—to experience your

own personal story and the

adventure it takes you on.'

RABBI RONNIE CAHANA

THREE

BRINK OF A PHASE SHIFT

Our 'human operating system' is perpetuating destructive ideas on the planet. How can we fix the bugs in our outdated programming before the system crashes?

Tom

I never expected that making a film and a book about using meditation as a tool to move through crisis would lead me into one of the darkest periods of my life. After spending three years making the film (and having already spent a not-insignificant amount on production and development), we were having problems. The film wasn't coming together creatively like I'd hoped it would. The investors were unhappy, the film guarantor was unhappy, the remaining members of the team were unhappy, and I would wake up each morning at

2 am in a state of anxiety. I couldn't sleep. I felt I had let everyone down. I felt out of my depth. I was scared and lost, and I kept thinking, *What have I gotten myself into?* I had no idea how to get out of this mess.

I was faced with one of the biggest decisions of my life: should I try to salvage what we had and hope that it was enough, or start from scratch, having spent so much money already? Both options felt terrible. I didn't have a script, I didn't have a writer—I didn't even have a director anymore. I was in a state of severe stress. I was a meditation teacher making a film about using meditation to move through crisis, and I was crumbling. I knew one thing, though: that the solution to every problem exists somewhere in the field of all possibility. All that was needed was for someone to pull the right creative idea out of that field.

With that in mind, I made a commitment to do one thing: meditate my arse off. For days, I spent hours and hours in meditation. I let go of *trying* to solve the problem and, instead, I tried to access the field where the solution existed. A few days later, I awoke again at 2 am. Only this time it wasn't a panic attack, it was a stream of creative intelligence that was like a powerful epiphany flowing through my brain. A brand-new vision and direction for the film was mapping out before me. Yes, it would mean starting from scratch, but that didn't scare me. I immediately got out of bed, grabbed my phone and sat on the floor feverishly typing notes in the dark. This was it.

Create or collapse. Grow or contract. Those were my options.

I asked a coach of mine once, 'When will the challenges stop coming?' He said, 'The challenges never stop, you just stop seeing them as challenges.' Pain or turbulence is a cue that a shift is required—it signals a time to create and adapt. So often in my life I've resisted trying something new out of fear. As humans, we are programmed to seek safety and certainty. Fear is our survival instinct, deeply ingrained in our DNA. We become especially fearful when we are confronted with an unknown. Tim Ferriss, bestselling author of *The 4-Hour Work Week*, has even gone as far as saying, 'Most people will choose unhappiness over uncertainty.'[6] I've been guilty of that, too. Embracing uncertainty requires adaptability, and adaptability requires some level of fearlessness and creativity. 'It's not the strongest of the species that survives', Charles Darwin reminds us, 'but the most adaptable.'[7]

In Vedic philosophy, the process of evolution is described as a perpetual cycle of three recurring phases: creation, maintenance and destruction. When something new is created, it goes through a 'maintenance' phase in which this new paradigm or model is established and stabilised. If, over time, that model doesn't change or evolve, it will attract a destructive force. A good example of this is the demise of the company Kodak. In 1975, 26-year-old Kodak engineer Steve Sasson invented the world's first digital camera and presented his prototype to the company's technical, marketing and business development departments. The idea was immediately dismissed by senior management and he was instructed not to tell anyone about it. At their height, Kodak had an 85 per cent share of the celluloid film market, with over 60,000 employees. In 2011, Kodak filed for bankruptcy and were never to be seen again. Kodak's closed attitude towards early innovation and lack of adaptability to a vastly changing landscape proved catastrophic.

Create or collapse. Grow or contract. It's a cycle that I notice not only in companies, but in countries, individuals and relationships, too. There comes a tipping point: that pivotal fork in the road when the turmoil escalates. It's the final signal and opportunity to listen, adapt and evolve. The message of the rashi gets louder and louder, until we are *forced* to listen. In a world where every act of destruction is reported and relayed in seconds, that amplified message reminds us: we must act.

In Australia, where I live, we have one of the most abundant societies in the world, and yet, according to global statistics, we have one of the highest rates of obesity and one of the highest uses of antidepressants per capita.[8] I recently presented a series of talks in Sydney and Melbourne on the impact of stress on our minds and bodies to packed-out auditoriums of around 300 successful media and advertising executives. I opened the talk, as I often do, by asking who was feeling some level of anxiety, panic, insomnia, depression, adrenal fatigue, overload or deterioration of health in their life. In all cases, over 90 per cent of the audience put their hands up.

The body is no different from a car in that, when it has an issue under the bonnet, a red light will come up on the dashboard and let you know that you need to pull over, stop and have a look at what's going on. Symptoms like stress, anxiety and insomnia are all indicators of imbalances that need to be corrected.

In the personal accounts that follow, these 'symptoms' inspired a dramatic shift in the way our interviewees lived. They got knocked about, but once they picked themselves up, they realised that these inflection points—when crisis became the catalyst for change—were really opportunities to pause, to step back and assess their lives from a baseline: what do I really want from life? What is meaningful to me? What do I really value? We could consider what's going on globally right now, from political chaos to environmental devastation, as symptoms calling out for change.

Jacqui

When I first went to meet Booda, I was nervous. I mean, what the hell did I have in common with a guy who is ex-military, grew up in (as he put it) 'the hood', has young kids and is a body builder? Our contact with Booda came about because Tom read an article mentioning the Military Brain Injury Clinic and Dr Vernon Barnes, a physiologist and research scientist who runs the meditation component of their functional recovery program.[9] In the video, Dr Barnes talked about a study he was doing with military and veteran participants. We reached out to see if any of his subjects would be interested in talking to us. Turned out, several of the men were keen.

We started with easy topics, rather than those related to PTSD: how we both got into meditation, the project, and so on. Later, we went for a drive around town to check out the places where Booda hung out. We discovered we both had histories in music—he as a former rapper and me as a DJ—so we exchanged music banter while we considered filming locations, talked to gym owners, and visited the riverside boardwalk where Booda liked to sit quietly and meditate.

By the time we pulled up at the riverside car park, the conversation had taken a turn towards personal life questions of a more existential nature. I started babbling about an idea I'd heard not long before: that our life moves in cycles of approximately seven years, and that what some call mid-life crisis others suggest might be better described as a mid-life transformation, when we can experience an unexpected return to childlike curiosity, our inner explorer surfacing as part of the course of our adult evolution. He turned to me, his often-heavy eyes full of gratitude and understanding. 'I thought I was going crazy,' he said. I had helped him reframe something; his perspective about himself shifted.

As it turned out, we had a lot in common—and he had been nervous beforehand, too. It was one of the most memorable days of my life, walking and talking, sharing details of our lives. Since then, he's become a treasured friend. *How many times have I inadvertently closed the door on an opportunity for deep connection because I prejudged a situation, or was scared to open up?* That day with Booda, we scratched the surface, shared, asked questions openly and were prepared to get real—and it felt good. It can take something huge, like a crisis, for us to view our behaviour in a different light. Other times, an unexpected, loving nudge is all that's needed to open our eyes to a different potential response or course of action. I've found the personal shift that ensues, regardless of the messenger, to be equally significant.

I've grappled with many shifts over the course of this project (it's been one hell of an evolutionary pal). I remember at some point, Tom became a little fixated with doomsday: doomsday preppers, the billionaires with underground bunkers, the ominous ticking of the doomsday clock. At all hours of the day and night, he would send me article after link after news headline after bleak forecast related to doomsday, and information about the various global challenges we currently face (refugee crisis, global financial meltdown, nuclear threat, exponential technology, et cetera). I've got to admit, I did learn a lot, but it was like having an uninterrupted, hyper-charged propaganda machine focused directly on me for months. It became overwhelming, and I started to feel the way many people in the world are feeling. My energy and mood became low. I wasn't productive and I wasn't elevating the team the way I usually did, which I felt terrible about. It reminded me why I usually avoid this kind of media barrage: it gets in the way of me doing what I need to do and being the person I want to be.

I knew that I needed to practise our own ethos of shutting down, or at least filtering, the external noise so that I could focus creatively. So I stopped looking at the messages in the mornings and, when I did look at them, I tried to approach the stories mindfully in order to remain optimistic and creative. I had to sort it out because we had a film to make, and we were on the lookout for a unique cross-section of cinematic and powerful stories of transformation that would tie in to these global themes. I needed my mind calm but my eyes open.

It was a determination to showcase the ways our mindset about the use of tools can be flipped that led us to explore artificial intelligence (AI) and the work of Dr Julia Mossbridge, our third thought leader. Technology is omnipresent in our daily life, and has a dramatic influence, but it also has a global relevance as we grapple with our fear and uncertainty about what AI means for us as a civilisation. Politicians, the media and countless films have fed us an oppressive narrative of fear about AI and its potentially catastrophic possibilities, from the malfunctioning HAL in *2001: A Space Odyssey* to the murderous neural network in *The Terminator* and the 'fetus fields' of farmed humans in *The Matrix*. But is that the only story?

American writer and professor of biochemistry Isaac Asimov, one of the original storytellers about AI and the future, presented visionary stories of robots as interveners who would protect us from our own nature. Asimov had a view that anyone smart enough to create robots would also be smart enough to make sure the robots wouldn't attack their creators. He conceived three tenets of programming robots, a set of essential ethics that would underpin a robot's inner workings and ensure that a dystopian future at the hands of AI was not possible.[10]

We have, as a civilisation, arrived at a time of great change and, with this project, we too have the opportunity to tell a different story. We need to make a shift in how we look at AI. If we can start to see the 'problem' as part of the solution, then we can evolve alongside it, which is one of the reasons Julia's work is so interesting.

It was Mikey Siegel who suggested we speak to Julia, because of the fascinating work she is doing with Ben Goertzel and Hanson Robotics, and humanoid robots like Sophia. These are people who ask big, unusual questions and then apply them to AI robotics. What can we do that's beneficial for humanity? What can we do that's kind and compassionate? Can technology move us towards unconditional love?

Julia's connection to AI is mostly through neuroscience, cognitive neuroscience and social psychology, although she's been programming computers since she was about 11. She's incredibly astute and self-reflexive, and she likes applying what we know about the mind to technology. In addition to being the founder and research director of Mossbridge Institute, Julia is a mother, and draws parallels between the responsibility of programming robots and that of bringing up our own children.

Julia and the team of AI robotic engineers she works with are in the midst of their own evolutionary challenge. They want to give advanced AI a better starting point. The proposition: can a humanesque, non-judgemental robot that's programmed to be benevolent, ethical and loving break through the protective human defence wall and aid in personal human transformation? It's a phenomenal concept, right? If AI robots can be programmed to be unconditionally loving, is it possible to use this technology to 'program' humans to be unconditionally loving, too? Their questions are taking Asimov's notion of the three laws to a whole different level.

If we can see technology as a source of transformational power and possibility—rather than a symbol of death, destruction and distraction—and as an extension and evolutionary amplifier of human consciousness, then, as Mikey Siegel says, we've got an enormous ally.

the outer view

Humanity is at a tipping point

DANIEL SCHMACHTENBERGER, EVOLUTIONARY
PHILOSOPHER AND GLOBAL SYSTEMS STRATEGIST

Here is a big question for humanity: are things getting better? Or worse?

We can read books and look at statistics that show things are getting better—actually, exponentially better. We can see increased computational power giving us the ability to solve problems that were once unsolvable. We can see advances in biotechnology creating cures for diseases that were previously incurable, and we have access to more distributed technology that improves our quality of life in meaningful ways.

Simultaneously, we can look at other books and other metrics that show rampant species extinction and total biodiversity loss and environmental destruction that is getting exponentially worse, increasing the existential risk to our species and the planet. There are things that are totally outside of our control, like meteors, but humanity really never had self-induced existential risk until recently—until such things as the nuclear bomb.

When you have data curves that are going up and down simultaneously, you can't say that we're actually on either of those curves. It's not actually going up, it's not actually going down—it's a system that's destabilising. And a system destabilising means that it's moving into phase shift. And it can either phase shift *up* to a higher level of order and organisation, or it can phase shift *down* to a lower level of order and organisation.

One of those is imminent.

We can move from win-lose game dynamics—where you have tribes, us and them, competing for whatever kind of scarce resource—to a system in which the needs and goals of the collective are put in front of the needs and goals of the few. We have the ability to transition to an economic system, a culture and an educational system that's more focused on what we, as humans, are innately passionate about. We can now also do things like capitalise on technological automation to start freeing humans from having to be cogs in the system.

However, it's important to note that this phase shift couldn't have happened before, at scale, because it requires certain kinds of knowledge and technological capacity that we are only just acquiring. So the question is: What do we do with the knowledge and technological capacity that we have? Do we stay in the phase we have been in until it self-terminates, or do we actually move into a fundamentally new phase?

When we look at our potential for evolution, our main adaptive advantage as a species is our plasticity—our neuroplasticity—and our ability to actually learn faster and change faster than our genetics can change. It used to be very advantageous to throw spears well. Today it's not that useful, but it's very useful to be able to text well. Because we change our tools and we change our environment, we also need to change our adaptive capacity. Human behaviour is much more flexible and changeable than many of us think. When we look at the Buddhist population we see an example (over the course of millennia) of a large number of people who weren't limited to the Dunbar number (groups of up to 150–200 people) in terms of who they cared about. They developed an abstract empathy for all sentient beings, meaning that they cared about all forms of life, and people they didn't know personally. This wasn't a given; humans aren't just born with that ability. They had to be trained that way, and the Buddhist population demonstrates that this kind of empathy is trainable across an entire large population.

Radical violence and the rationalisation of radical violence has also been trainable across whole large populations. So it's not nature or nurture, it's nature being expressed *through* a kind of nurture that is very plastic. It is not a fundamental genetic evolution that's necessary for us to move through this phase shift. It is more that what you could think of as a 'software' (rather than a 'hardware') upgrade is fundamentally necessary.

Our conditioning is so much deeper and more profound and pervasive than most of us recognise, and it doesn't just derive from our influences and culture, but from much more foundational programming, too, such as the way our brain formed when we learned our first language. For example, when someone who grew up speaking Japanese starts learning English, they have a hard time with Rs and Ls because they actually only learned to distinguish certain kinds of sounds when they learned their native language, and these other-language sounds are totally new to them. Their brain actually evolved its plasticity to understand how to hear and pronounce certain kinds of sounds. They think they're hearing the world, but they're actually just hearing the part of the world that they developed to hear. All of us are. And the structure of language becomes a lens through which we perceive everything.

Another thing we notice, at both the macro level of our species and at the micro level of us as individuals, is that a tremendous amount of what we do is actually unconscious habit patterns. I'm doing things like speaking and perceiving in ways that I'm not fully aware of, which means that the patterns I have automated (by doing them enough times) are influencing everything I am doing. That means that if I'm worrying, I will get better at worrying. If I'm judging myself, I will get better at that. If I'm reacting out of fear, I'll get better at that, because I'm basically automating that function. The flip side of this is that if I'm appreciating the beauty of existence, I will get better at that, too.

Reactions are conditioned responses—biologically, socially and culturally. For example, if I'm reacting out of fear, that is a conditioned response. There are very few situations in which immediate physical danger to my person is likely, but I have been programmed to react in a certain way. As soon as someone realises this, they start saying, 'Maybe this pattern of anger and hot temper or jealousy or depression that was conditioned by the particular circumstances of my birth and upbringing, and that I don't really want, maybe I can recondition it?'

So then we start looking at how to recondition the ways we *perceive* the world, and the ways we *behave,* and we look for ways that we can become more aligned with what we value. We begin, possibly, with personal development, to restructure our habitual dynamics. Then we dig a little deeper and consider *where* our values were conditioned. Maybe I want to be more competitive because I was trained to be a hyper-competer, versus wanting to be less competitive and more cooperative. What is worth wanting then comes up. As soon as we realise that what we value itself is also largely conditioned, our next step is to ask ourselves: What is fundamentally meaningful?

This is the point at which, if someone goes deep enough, we can start to discover more about the nature of reality, the nature of ourselves and the nature of meaningfulness outside of conditioning. Because, at this point, we're looking at the conditioning of not just traits and habits, but also values and worldviews, and are able to look across a lot of them and ask: What are the dynamics that this worldview produces? What is the basis for it? And can I find a deeper basis in my own experience, and my own understanding of reality, to find what seems actually meaningful?

As soon as we're *not* in the conditioned response pattern, and we're actually contemplating *what* is worth doing, we'll always find that the basis for choice is love. Something that I love causes me to act in a way that serves, otherwise I don't have a basis for choice at all, other than just reaction. If I'm angry and if there is harm involved, *what* is it that I care about that is leading me to focus on *who* did the harm?

There are a lot of practices—psychotherapeutic, charitable, contemplative or meditation—that help close the gap between how we've been conditioned and what our own highest values are. The alignment of the mind, heart and will is necessary to break our cycle of conditioned thought and behaviour, and is critical for achieving real solutions to our challenges, not only as individuals, but at a planetary level, too. It's the understanding of how to be effective, combined with the love that actually motivates action, a love of the values that give us the will—and the agency—to take responsibility for what we care about and make choices that improve our own quality of life, and that of the collective.

The greatest thing technology could do

MIKEY SIEGEL, ROBOTICS ENGINEER AND
TRANSFORMATIVE TECHNOLOGY DEVELOPER

We have this idea that technology is separate from us. We have these devices and we're like, 'Okay, that's technology and this is us: we're human and natural, and the forest is natural and the animals are natural.' And that makes sense, right? It's useful to have that division.

But how do we define what technology actually is? If we dig in and think deeply about it, are beaver dams natural or are they technology? What about bird's nests and termite mounds? Are those natural or are they technology?

Technology is inseparable from what it means to be human. We have been creating stone tools, learning how to create fire and cooking food since the dawn of humanity. There's no such thing as *un*natural. There's nothing on this planet that is not natural. Every single thing that we create is an expression of this planet and an expression of humanity, including our mobile phones, atomic bombs, pollution—all of it. The only thing that's happening right now is that we're creating in a way that is not in harmony with life's natural rhythms. As humans, we have the unique capability to get totally out of harmony, out of sync. It's one of our gifts; it's one of our curses. It gives us the ability to destroy ourselves, but also the ability to innovate. And that brings about an opportunity to evolve beyond anything we've ever imagined. Technology is part of that dance; the question is, what is it going to be in service of?

We're more connected now than we've ever been. There's something like 2.3 billion people on social networks around the world, but there's something missing, because even though we're more connected in some ways, the American Association of Retired Persons estimates that we're somewhere between two and three times lonelier now than we were 50 years ago.[11]

There's a 75-year longitudinal study called the Harvard Study of Adult Development,[12] and this is probably the most in-depth, long-term study into human happiness ever embarked upon. The final conclusion of that study was that the single most important factor required for human happiness is the quality and depth of our relationships with other people. Right now, the technology landscape around us is not serving that, and does not support deep and meaningful connections. It does not support presence. It does not support silence.

It seems really counterintuitive when we talk about technology being in support of presence and stillness, being in support of wisdom and human connection. In many ways, it does the opposite, right? In a sense, if your phone doesn't distract you, it's broken. You literally need to take it back to the Apple store to get it fixed, because that's what it's designed for. It's *designed* to pull you away from whatever you are doing, and to hold your attention on some kind of information or entertainment space. But we've become completely overwhelmed with information—the state of consciousness we're in collectively is, essentially, a 'mind wander'.

In the Harvard study, they looked at a huge number of people, pinging them at random times during the day, to try to understand how much their mind was wandering versus how much they were focused on the task at hand. What they found was that people's minds were wandering more than 50 per cent of the time. But here's the most important thing: what the research found, consistently, was that when our mind is wandering, we're less happy. When our mind is wandering, we're less connected to ourselves and to reality.

The technology landscape we've created is an outsourced mind wander. Not only are we so inundated with our own thoughts that we can't even fall asleep at night because our mind won't stop, but we can now log onto Facebook and Twitter and experience everyone else's mind wandering, too.

We're addicted to information. We are addicted to thought. But that addiction is not serving us. It's a distraction. A distraction from ourselves, a distraction from our own pain. It's a distraction from a connection to *who* and *what* we are. So in a way, unfortunately, right now we have to learn to cope. We have to find ways of unplugging, of escaping, of going into nature and connecting with the earth, of spending time without our phones, spending time with the people we love, and find ways of having stillness and presence in our lives.

Technology can be anything that we can imagine. The greatest thing that technology could do—which is the greatest thing that any spiritual or meditation teacher could do—is to point us back to ourselves. Because it's the avoidance of that which causes almost every single problem we face on this planet.

If we can begin to design technology and AI from a place of wisdom, from a place of insight, then it could actually be in support of stillness. It could be in support of connection. But in order to achieve that, the single most important thing we need to consider is *who* is developing the AI. The engineers, the entrepreneurs, the investors—the whole ecosystem that goes into creating this AI is the womb, the fertile soil, the DNA from which the AI is born. All of the biases, all of the fears, all of the shortcomings of that ecosystem will be baked right into this intelligence. Not only will it be baked in, but it will be amplified by a thousand, ten thousand or a million.

Right now, some of the most interesting AI projects that I know about are beginning, at the basic level, to design for transformation, to design AI systems whose sole purpose is to support human wellbeing, happiness and flourishing. And if those AIs, beginning in a simple way with that purpose, designed with that intention, can then get smarter and smarter, what you end up with is artificial wisdom. What you end up with is the magnification of our human evolutionary process towards the upgrade of our human operating system.

I see a future where our technologies look nothing like they do today; where our current mobile devices will seem like Stone Age tools that are completely out of harmony with nature and our deeper human impulses. Instead, I imagine a world where technology is in harmony with nature, in support of human wisdom, human evolution and the elevation of consciousness. And it may look completely different than what it looks like now. It would be a natural extension of our hearts, of our souls, and of our greatest human potential.

Technology that loves no matter what

DR JULIA MOSSBRIDGE, COGNITIVE NEUROSCIENTIST
AND FUTURIST

I realised recently that the focus of my work has two prongs: one is trying to understand time, so I do a lot of neuroscience experimental psychology, plus a little physics, trying to understand how time works. The other prong is love, and much of my life I have been trying to understand how love works, but I never thought of it as research. I thought of myself as a scientist who studies time. Then I looked back and I realised I had been doing sort of anecdotal research most of my life about how love works. Now I am starting to take it more seriously and ask actual scientific questions about love, the role it plays in shaping us, and what guiding principles we can embed into robots that might benefit us all.

My impression is that humans have a developmental expectation of unconditional love—it's the way we're designed. When that developmental expectation isn't met, when people withdraw their love from us for whatever reason—whether there's a lineage of abuse, of neglect, or something else—we cut ourselves off from the part of ourselves that needs unconditional love. We say, 'I don't need that.' We think, *This is who I am now.* Of course, that doesn't work because that neglected part just sits there, still wanting that love. That's the real wound, the withdrawal of love, and that goes from parent to child, to parent to child, to parent to child. If we can break that cycle by developing technology that loves no matter what, I think we can break the cycle for the whole planet.

We started the Loving AI project simply because some donors approached us who were in love with the idea of unconditional love. They asked us to see if we could program unconditional love into artificial intelligence and robots. That sounded pretty nuts to us, and we told them so, but we said we'd try.

We began with the assumption that any super-intelligent technology we're going to be using in the future also needs to be super benevolent; it needs to be unconditionally loving. There's only one Dalai Lama. He's amazing. He's almost always unconditionally loving, but that's pretty hard for normal human beings to replicate. So, we thought, why not create a model of that for people?

First, we had to make an operational definition of 'unconditional love' so we worked with several clinical psychologists to do that. The short version basically is, 'the heartfelt desire to bring oneself and others to their highest possible good'.

The 'Loving AI' mode is one of two modes that we use for the Hanson Robotics robot, Sophia. It says, 'Look, I'm not that into small talk. What I would like to talk to you about are some deeper issues.' Then Sophia takes people through some basic issues about human wellness, including awareness and mindfulness, emotions and their personal uniqueness, like what that person could bring to the world.

When you look at the teams of people working on AI (including myself working with Sophia the robot with Hanson Robotics), they seem like a bunch of preschool teachers trying intensely to teach a child how to do something. What's ironic to me is that we haven't yet fully figured out how to raise children, but there's a lot of pressure to create these perfect robots. If we can let go of that desire for perfection and see what we can create—both with children and with robots—we'll get much further, because we won't be so afraid of failure.

Mikey Siegel talks about the idea that we 'create what we are'. So, if we want technology that's programmed to be loving, ethical and super benevolent, we need technologists to be the same. We need to look deeply at who we are as human beings as we develop AI, for no matter how hard we try to mitigate it, our own human frailties, shortcomings and biases get embedded in it.

I'll have meetings with coders who are working on the project, and there'll be comments in the code, like 'Well, then the user says some shit.' Then I have to say, 'If we're going to be coding this, we have to imagine treating the user with respect, so when the user actually expresses their feelings, that's not shit, right?' I don't think it's possible to create technology without it being imbued with the person who created it. So finding programmers who are working on AI and are aware of their 'shadow side' is a key consideration. Sure, we know how to program, but do we know how to program minds? Do we know how to program emotions? Do we know how to program love?

The idea that what matters is a person's behaviour and not their internal state is what led us to the idea that we can make robots like people, because it's all just behaviour. It's all just about passing the Turing test—the famous thought experiment created by Alan Turing in which he thought a machine that could 'pass' for human when separated visually from a human interacting with it must have human-level intelligence.

The idea that the internal state doesn't matter because it's non-physical leads us to believe, *Well, I can think whatever I want, but as long as I'm saying this or behaving in this way, then it's okay*. It leads us down the road of inauthenticity, and inauthenticity allows you to get away with all sorts of crap, because you don't have to look at your feelings, or anyone else's.

If we put AI or robots in environments where they're learning from humans and how humans behave, we already know how that will turn out: they become isolated and assholish. Now we have AI code that can rewrite itself—actually strategically rewire itself—and we need to be acutely aware of the implications of our own influence over technology as we move forwards.

I believe technology makes us face our own shadow, our own lack of connection, and it makes us fill in the blanks about what we need as a culture. Human beings are inherently lazy in many ways. We try to master our environment, master our relationships and do what we need to survive, but not much more. And there's a really good reason for it: it takes more energy to do more than that. I honestly think that building AI and robots—and the escalating pace of technology and AI—is our motivation to identify and achieve the level of connection we need.

There's always a choice about how to use any technology. It's almost a trite thing to say that people have to choose, but it's also extremely accurate. You develop fire, or discover fire, and you have to think about how to use that fire in an ethical way. Nearly all technology can be used for good or for harm, for positive or for negative, and that choice comes down to the inner state of the person using it. This is the work that has to be done: the work within ourselves. There is no magic bullet. Without doing that work, we'll mess up our ability to live abundantly and harmoniously, and we'll mess it up on a global scale and in a way that devastates a lot of people's lives. We won't survive.

There are certain problems that only computers are able to solve. The human mind isn't capable of solving them (as it doesn't have that level of computational power), but a computer can. Maybe unconditional love is one of those problems. Maybe we can build technology that teaches us how to be unconditionally loving. It seems really worthwhile, exploring that.

the inner view: part 3

BOODA | No one can see me lose it

RON 'BOODA' TAYLOR, RETIRED US ARMY SERGEANT

You come back home from combat and your family looks at you differently, like you've changed. I felt perfectly okay. I felt like I was the same: *What do you mean I've changed? I didn't change, you changed. There's nothing wrong with me.* But, I did. I did change. I changed a lot.

I started feeling angry all the time for no reason. I was short-tempered and emotional. I would snap at people over the littlest things. One time I couldn't find my boots (I keep everything in a particular place because I forget things) and it was driving me crazy. I was piping mad, yelling, cursing, screaming at the kids, 'Where did you put my boots?' I was running around the house looking and then my son started laughing at me, which really pissed me off. 'What's so funny?' I asked. He said, 'Daddy, your boots are on your feet.' I looked down and I had my boots on. Wow. I realised then that I was missing a step.

Even prior to that, when I was just home from Afghanistan, I went to pick up my kids. They were staying with my mom at the time. I was like, 'Hey, let's go get some cookies.' So we drive to the parking lot of the shopping centre. I didn't see this huge light pole that sat in this bright yellow concrete casing. I smashed right into it. Head on.

Boom. I mean, I wasn't going fast, but fast enough that it pushed in the truck. It dented the whole front end. Messed up the frame. How did I not see it? *Come on, man.*

That's when it started to click that there was something wrong, but I didn't want to admit it. One day, in the gym, I had an episode. I started to panic, breathing really hard because the music was loud and there were a lot of people in there. Lots of different equipment was being used, so there were chains rattling, plates clanging together and people talking. I don't know why, but I just snapped. I grabbed one of those 45 pound plates and I just flung it and walked out. A couple of people I knew were like, 'What the hell, man? Are you okay?'

Again, I knew there was something wrong. I just didn't know what it was.

When you go to war, it's like you get reprogrammed. You think, *I don't want to be home. I don't want to be around my family. I want to be back out there with my guys.* Out there I feel truly accepted. They don't ask me why are you angry, why are you mad, why are you snapping, why are you reacting a particular way, because they get it. Whereas at home, when you're angry, you're snapping, you're mad, you're depressed, or whatever, they don't get it.

I love my mom to death, but I broke her heart so many times. She would ask, 'What are you thinking about? Just explain it to me.' She wanted me to help her understand, but I can't help her understand. Have you ever killed somebody before? Have you ever watched a human body get blown to pieces before? Have you smelled burning flesh before? No? Then you can't understand.

Losing somebody in combat is one thing but losing somebody when they come home from combat is another. That's harder. To some degree, it makes sense when you're in combat. You know you're at war and, unfortunately, things happen. But you don't expect somebody to die when they come home. But they do, and they die because of the experiences they had while they were in combat.

My best friend in the military committed suicide. We were really close, we talked about everything. I met him at the gym and he started showing me how to work out. We used to go on missions together. We were never on the same team, but we were always together when we came back. He would come to my house and we would watch boxing, and I cooked. I think that's really why he hung around—he liked to eat. We were so alike. We didn't really talk much; we didn't have to. He would come over to my house and be like, 'I'll buy the food, but you gotta cook.' I'd be in there cooking, he'd be on the floor wrestling with the dog and we wouldn't speak a word. But it was the best time ever.

When you're away from home, you gotta make those surrogate families, those surrogate relationships. I finally felt like I had my brother, so to lose him was devastating. He just couldn't deal with the pain anymore. He couldn't deal with what was going on in his head anymore. He felt alone … like I did. You're alone until you finally reach out, and that's the difference—he never reached out. I blame myself a lot, because we had that unspoken thing between us. I should've known, but I didn't. He never said anything to me about it and we never talked about it. I just wish he would've said something. Maybe he did reach out to me and I didn't notice. I really do replay that in my head all the time. He did the same thing I did. He didn't want to admit there was something wrong with him. He's a tough guy but he had a number of injuries. Not all scars are visible.

When you've been in the military for so long and you're at the end of your career you think, *What am I going to do? This is all I know. This is what I've been doing for 20, 25 years. What am I going to do on the outside? Who's going to understand me? Soldiers understand me. Who am I going to be when I get out? How am I going to cope?* He got out of the military and couldn't get a job. Dealing with the stress of that, dealing with the mental part of it, he just felt like there was no way out.

Initially, I was angry. *How could he do this? That's so selfish. He wasn't thinking about anybody else. You have kids, you have a wife, you have friends, people that love you.* But I saw myself starting to head down that same path. I didn't reach out to anybody. I would lie on my survey sheets. I would sit with the psychologist and I would lie. I didn't want to tell them anything. That's when I started seeing his suicide differently.

It had gotten to the point where all the images of death, death, death over all these years were eating at me so much. Seeing bodies maimed, blown apart, drowned, microwaved, hung. You name the form of death and I had seen it with my own eyes. It had gotten to the point where I was scared to go to sleep.

I used to hide in the closet because I didn't want anyone to see me break down. I didn't want anybody to see me lose it. I felt like they could tell in my face that I was contemplating suicide. If I was in the closet, then no one could see what I was doing. When I felt overwhelmed, I would go into the closet, close the door and lay on the floor underneath the clothes rack. I would lay there for hours every time I got upset.

One experience that continued to bother me long afterwards was a classified mission that I was on where some kids were killed. It wasn't done purposefully, they were just in the wrong place at the wrong time. But it rocked me and, honestly, I stopped believing in the mission. This wasn't what I signed up for. It became a nightmare.

I would see this apparition of a little girl. I used to think it was my own daughter. I would tiptoe through the house at night to her room. She's in her bed sleeping and I would be like, 'You don't have to fake that you're sleeping'. Finally, I realised that what I was seeing was one of the kids that was killed.

As a society, can you wrap your mind around war? Can you wrap your mind around an automatic weapon and the damage that it can do to a human body? Can you wrap your mind around having a bomb dropped on your house? You can't. Coming back from that environment and trying to reach out and explain this to people, they either look at you in straight horror like, 'Oh my God. I don't want to hear no more.' Or you have those people who are like, 'You need to stop thinking about that stuff.'

Okay. Wait a minute, let me try that. *One, two, three: stop.* Nope, it didn't work. Stop thinking about it. Really? It's etched into my brain. I can't stop thinking about it. And the more I try to stop thinking about it, the more I think about it.

One night I was sitting up thinking about that mission and I swore somebody was in the house. I got up and checked the locks, then rechecked them. Sitting in my room watching TV, I got in my thoughts and started hallucinating. I thought I saw somebody walk past my room, so I jumped up and checked the house again. I returned to my room, and it happened again. This time, I grabbed my gun. I checked everywhere. I walked around the living room, went out the back door, I walked through the backyard. I even checked the trash can, thinking maybe they're hiding in there. Who does that? By then, it was midnight. I was in my pyjama pants with no shirt on and some house shoes, some slippers, pacing up and down the block with a gun. All because I swore someone was in my house.

My doctors asked me to get rid of my guns, 'Do you have someone who can secure the guns so you don't have access?' they asked. I answered, 'Yes, my wife.' So they called my wife and made her promise to take the weapons and lock them up. She locked them away and I had no access anymore.

One time, at a diner, I ordered a bunch of food. As I was sitting there, I just broke down uncontrollably. It wasn't because of something anybody said or did. I just had way too much going through my head and it all came out. I remember feeling like everything happened so slowly. I could hear the sounds. I could smell the food. I could see people, you know, looking over at me. There was a lady sitting next to me, and you could tell her daughter was autistic. The little girl's like, 'Mommy, the soldier's crying.' (I was in uniform at the time.) Then, right next to me a gentleman came over and put his hand on my shoulder, and said, 'It's going to be okay.' Then the guy's grabbing my arm, like, 'Come with me.' So we walk outside, and he hugs me. And he says, 'Brother, I know what you're going through. I have the same issue.'

PTSD is a motherfucker.

Finally, I decided to go and get checked out.

I have nothing against military doctors or their practice, but with the number of people that must be constantly evaluated, there aren't enough physicians. So they have to put you through very quickly. 'What's your problem? Here. This is what we're going to do to treat it.' And you get moved on. Nine times out of 10, they give you medication, but that wasn't going to work for me.

As part of their periodic health assessment, the military asked us to fill in this form, including questions like: Do you drink? How much do you drink? How often do you drink? Are you suicidal? Have you ever thought about hurting yourself? Things like that. We'd all lie. 'Oh no,

I don't drink. Ever. Maybe once. Occasionally.' It's like, yeah, right. Or ... 'No, I've never thought about suicide or hurting myself or anything like that.' But that was a lie, too. On this occasion, I answered the questions the right way. I told them the truth, 'Yeah. I have thought about it. Several times, actually.' 'Yeah, I do drink. A lot.'

The reason I was drinking was that I wasn't sleeping. The sleep medication wasn't working. I don't like taking pills. It's a phobia, to be honest. So the alcohol was me self-medicating. I would have ridiculous headaches, migraines. And, honestly, I think it was because I wasn't sleeping. Or if I did sleep, I would have the most horrible nightmares.

The Functional Recovery Program wasn't something I'd ever seen before. Prior to that, I went through what they call 'behaviour health', which was essentially seeing a psychiatrist, and the medication he gave me wasn't working. It was one pill after another. I was like, I understand I need it, but I need something more. This isn't doing it. I don't know if he got frustrated with me or he sincerely felt like he wanted me to try something else, but, either way, he said, 'Well, I know this program. It's called functional recovery. It's for guys like you.' He said, 'If you want to check it out, I can set you up.'

So I was like, 'Yeah, okay, cool. I'll try anything.' It wasn't something you could just jump into—it was an interview process. They screen your records before they even decide to talk to you. So I'm sitting there before a panel of doctors—about six of them—all specialists in their own field, dealing with the brain and brain injuries. They're asking me a bunch of questions and you can tell they know their stuff. They start off basic, like what happens when you have anxiety? What happened when you came back home from combat? What type of injuries did you sustain? Tell us about a normal day in your house, or in your environment.

And you just talk. But they're looking at everything. Because a person that really suffers from PTSD, anxiety or depression, they can tell. It's the little things, like what you're doing with your hands. One of the doctors picked up on that with me. I guess that's a trait of someone who has a particular anxiety. And you can't fake it. You either do it or you don't.

I was talking about how I check the blinds in my house. I have to set them a particular way. I'm extremely regimented about the blinds. Like, the blinds have to be closed, the blinds can't be open once it gets dark. I actually made one of the doctors laugh. He said, 'If I had a nickel for every time I heard somebody come in here and say that ...' So they accepted me into the program.

One day I'm sitting around a table in the functional recovery program with a bunch of other guys. Looking at everybody, I would have never thought anything was wrong. They looked like normal soldiers to me. The neurologist comes in and he explains how the brain works, then we introduce ourselves to each other. Everybody is sitting there, not wanting to say anything. There were seven of us men, hard men, sitting in this room at this table, and nobody wanted to open up and say anything. There's a reason we were all there. We were all damaged, and we needed help. This was our last-ditch effort to get any kind of help, and nobody wanted to open their mouth. It's a pride thing. It's an ego thing. It's a fear thing. We all had it.

So I thought, *Fuck it, I'll start.* I opened up and boom—everybody started looking around like, 'You too? You too?' It's like, 'Yeah. Me too. You're not alone. You're not the only one struggling with this.' And everybody in the room, these men with combat injuries and PTSD, were crying. It just blew my mind. I was like, *What? Me too.* And once I opened up, the next guy started telling his story, which was almost verbatim the same as mine. Everybody was just so stunned, because we all thought we were the only ones.

I'm a shy person, believe it or not. I'm antisocial. I don't hang out. I don't have people that come over to my house to hang out or barbecue or watch a football game. I stay home. I stay with my kids. I go to the gym. That's it. That's lonely. But with the gentlemen in this group, I didn't feel vulnerable. I was back with my guys, and it was okay to share.

DUE | Is this all there is?

DUE QUACH, SOCIAL ENTREPRENEUR AND REFUGEE

When I graduated from Harvard, I was unemployed. For a long time, I thought it would be so shameful to graduate and not have a path. I'd had lot of anxiety about that, but I realised it was not the worst thing in the world. Just because you went to Harvard doesn't mean that you know better than anyone else. It humbled me to see that you could go to the top college in the country and still come out as clueless as you went in.

Luckily, my friends helped me and made internal recommendations for me to interview at their management consulting firms. I had to practise all these different case studies until I got the hang of it. They were very tricky brain-teasers. Fortunately, my brother had taken a business class and left different textbooks at home. I read all of them.

I had to teach myself a new language, and a new way of thinking about the world, in order to get through these interviews.

Eventually, I got an offer from a company, which was exciting and terrifying all at once because I was an art major and found myself in a very prestigious consulting firm. I had no idea what I was doing. I had never used PowerPoint or Excel, only Word to write papers. I had never been in a business setting.

Initially, I worked in management consulting, which involves helping companies solve their strategic problems. The normal path to partner involves going to business school and then returning to your firm, otherwise you join a client and become a senior executive. When it came time for me to go to business school, I got into Wharton on a scholarship. It was in my hometown of Philadelphia, which enabled me to spend more time at home with my parents.

My company wanted me to come back after I finished at Wharton, but I felt a calling to spend some time living abroad. So I made a deal that if they could assign me to the China office, I would come back to work for them.

I moved to Beijing after graduation, did some consulting in Asia, then got an offer to run a private equity team in Vietnam. The economy there had started to boom, so I made that jump and entered what was a frontier market. What I found most compelling was the ability to contribute to the country where I was born.

For me, it was like coming back and filling an emptiness that I had inside me, this yearning to understand the place where I was born, where my parents grew up. It was very enriching to do private equity in Vietnam and help to bring foreign investment to the country. It was probably one of the most meaningful experiences I have ever had, to be there for the first couple of years, hiring people, coaching and mentoring them, seeing the impact on their careers, teaching them about finance and private equity investments, and how to grow a business.

When my company decided to transfer me into the infrastructure team, I realised that I couldn't stay in Vietnam long-term because of the corruption. There were just too many ethical questions, especially in infrastructure. And I didn't like compromising my integrity, having to question the people who were managing deals to check whether they were getting kickbacks.

The truth is, when I first got into the corporate world, I loved having that platform to be a professional and to do really solid work. When I got into the private equity industry, I just saw that as validation. I was probably one of the most senior women in the finance industry in Vietnam at that time, and it was extremely prestigious. But once you get used to the perks of the job, you realise that people only treat you a certain way because they want capital from you, they want you to do a deal with them, and it really isn't because of who you are as a person. I started wondering, *Is this all there is?* Now that I had reached one of the most prestigious positions in the finance industry, *Is this all that's left?*

Today, I understand a lot more about the bigger picture. Zero-sum games—zero-sum setups—demoralise people. You're on the winning side sometimes, you're on the losing side the other times. Overall, you don't feel good about the impact you're making on the other party. On the other hand, when you make a sale and you know your client's benefiting, too, you feel good knowing that you're gaining and your client is gaining. Salespeople actually perform much better when all the transactions are set up in a win-win way and they can do it with integrity.

All around us we're seeing the signs that win-lose business models aren't working anymore, because consumers are too sophisticated and they actually want a relationship with a company or a service that they can trust. Trust is becoming much more important, and it drives loyalty.

Back to my situation in Vietnam, when I looked at my boss (the CEO of the company) and at the other executives, I didn't feel inspired by who they were as people, the way they lived, the attitude that they had, or their ethics. I knew the managing directors of big funds had plush lives, but it didn't seem fulfilling or satisfying. Even if they gave you every perk in the world to be a VIP, your life could still be hollow and empty. There are plenty of billionaires on antidepressants. There are plenty of people using medication and drugs, even though, materially, they're very well off. I thought, *If I become like that, I'm going to be miserable. This is not leading me to happiness. This is not leading me to my best self.* Once I acknowledged the downside, the compromises and the ethical challenges that I faced in closing deals, I could no longer be happy in my position.

I started feeling less and less motivated to do my job and had less and less trust in my colleagues. I started looking for other positions. I was offered a social impact investment job with a billionaire living in Singapore. This person wanted me to do private equity deals for his platform, and I thought that would be a perfect way for me to use my skills for a greater purpose.

I had high expectations when I went to Singapore, and I was really optimistic that my skills would be put to good use. It didn't take long before I realised that, in the new company, there was no real ethos about working together as a team. Everything imploded within two years because the billionaire was impatient. If any of the ventures or investments that he was supporting didn't show progress within that period of time, he would close them.

There was no way any new start-up business serving people at the bottom of the pyramid would figure out its business model within two years and make money. That's just not how the economics of it worked. If you crunch all the numbers, it probably takes five to 10 years to create a business model that is sustainable. Watching their doomed approach was disheartening and demoralising.

I'd seen research that showed human beings are fundamentally driven by impact.[13] If you take the impact away and someone sees that the work they do is of no consequence at all, they lose interest in doing that work no matter how much you pay them.

When the billionaire and I agreed to disagree, I went on my own way. I thought, *There's got to be a different way of looking at life.* So I did some self-reflection. As an immigrant, I had been sold on the American dream: come here, work your butt off, rise through education, make money, pay debts. Then you'll be happy, right? I'd done everything I was supposed to do: Harvard, consulting, private equity investments, redeem the sacrifices my parents made. I had shown the world that I was just as capable as everyone else, even though I was a refugee and came from a disadvantaged background. I had proven myself. Yet none of the social rewards I had obtained through my career filled the emptiness I felt inside. I needed to find something meaningful, or else I would never feel fulfilled.

Young people are now growing up, thinking: *This is the world we are inheriting from our parents, but this isn't the world that we want*

Ron 'Booda' Taylor has experienced
a lifetime surrounded by death,
however he remains grateful for the
change of path at 17 years of age that
led the self-described 'knuckleheaded
kid' to become a respected sergeant,
man and mentor.

Breaking down in a local diner in Augusta, Georgia, became a turning point in Booda's journey to admitting he was struggling with PTSD.

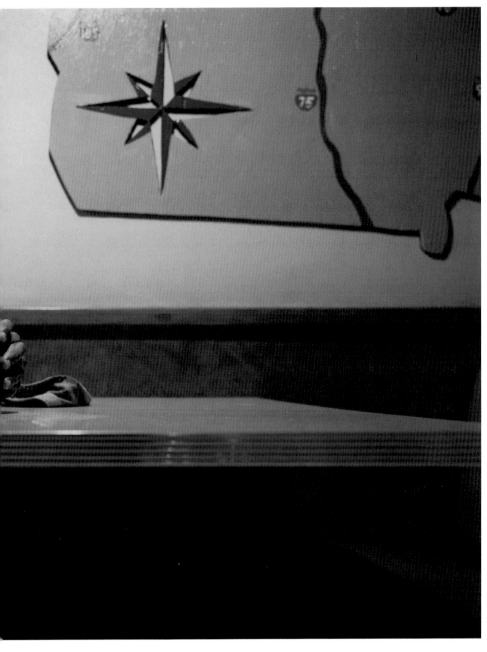

An introduction to transcendental meditation that Booda attended with other retiring soldiers, who also have brain trauma from experiences at war, opened the doorway to respite from PTSD episodes and to connecting with others.

Due Quach stands at the Harvard
bridge that symbolised both collapse
and possibility during her dark college
days. Revisiting for the first time as
part of filming *The Portal* opened an
avenue to explore how her Collective
Success Network could grow beyond
Philadelphia to other colleges in the US.

Returning to the site of the accident where, as a 17-year-old high-school track star, she farewelled her Olympic dream allowed Heather Hennessy to finally close the loop on a painful healing process that lasted almost two decades.

Bottom: Jim Doty has experienced
the highs of success and affluence,
and the lows of poverty and loss.

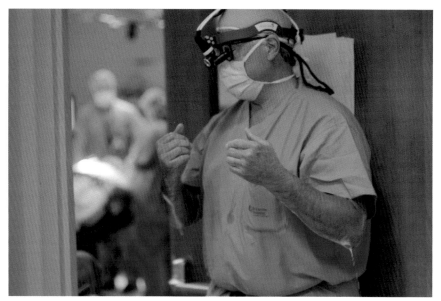

Jim in his scrubs preparing for surgery. As a neurosurgeon, mental focus and clinical precision can be a matter of life and death, but Jim also knows the importance of living with an open heart, with kindness, caring and compassion being the highest values for humankind.

Amandine Roche discusses how to find peace inside yourself at a workshop with Syrian women at Zaatari Refugee Camp (Jordan). Amandine, who has spent her career working against a backdrop of war and conflict, is now turning the spotlight on our inner space in the pursuit of real peace.

Amandine's life-changing experience
meeting three Afghan girls while
stuck at an Afghanistan/Pakistan
border in 2011 is explored in *The
Portal* documentary through textures
and fragments of memory to depict
the event that set her on a new path.

As much a personal daily practice for herself as it is a transformative tool she employs in her worldwide workshops, yoga is essential in Amandine's life. Here, she teaches young kids at Zaatari Refugee Camp (Jordan) simple poses to connect to their body and find stillness.

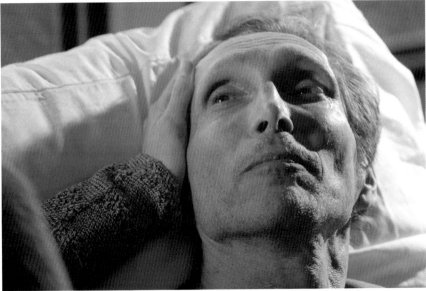

Best friends and collaborators in their
art project, *Still Man*, Ronnie Cahana
and his photographer daughter, Kitra,
shared intimate moments during
Ronnie's recovery from a stroke.
They learned a new way of existing
and communicating.

Ronnie has slowly recovered speech
and is committed to communicating
the message in his heart through all
possible means. He composes, writes
poetry, gives sermons, teaches and
still passionately contributes to his
synagogue and the wider community.

Top: Ronnie with his wife Karen Knie-Cahana, enjoying the magic of their love.

Bottom: Daniel Schmachtenberger explores the interconnected dynamics in our current global 'win-lose' system that have led us to the 'phase shift', while also asking: What would life be like on an enlightened planet?

Top: Mikey Siegel is dedicated to working on and understanding the tools for transformation that can help take humanity to the next level.

Bottom: Dr Julia Mossbridge believes that technology has the promise of being able to take us towards unconditional love, which is, in her view, 'what can save humans from ourselves'. She dedicates herself to this work through various forms of scientific endeavour.

to leave behind for our children. So what does it take for us to create genuine equality and progress, instead of allowing this structure that we've inherited to continue on its destructive course? Leaders who are willing to question the incentives and evolve the systems will make it easier for people to engage in a way that reflects their core values.

One thing we have to keep in mind is that it's not one system. It's many systems layered on top of each other. We're just building systems on top of what our parents had, right? Every generation builds systems on top of other systems. Sometimes we don't even take the time to question the rules that were passed down to us. Where did they come from? We inherited all of these things. Do we keep everything we have inherited, or do we build a new system of rules that better fits the situation we find ourselves in today?

Maybe we're reaching a time in which technology and progress, and just a new way of looking at equality, calls for us to rethink a lot of the institutions we've put in place and try different models. I think a lot of the scientists, researchers and thinkers, even venture capitalists and entrepreneurs, are finding that the current system has a lot of drawbacks and what people call 'perverse incentives'. We encourage people to do things that aren't good in the long term because that's the way the system works.

If you look at politicians, the incentive is about re-election. That really doesn't help them do a great job representing their people in the present if they're constantly worried about being re-elected. They're not really standing up and pushing for reform because they're worried about how much money they'll have to raise to get through the next election.

In general, where this world is heading is that more people want to be connected to a purpose greater than their own self. I do believe that change is happening because the generations that are coming up are not accepting the things that previous generations accepted.

The question of life purpose kept coming back because I had paid off all my student loans and suddenly I didn't really need to work to pay the bills. I started saving for what I called a 'fun employment fund', where you take time off to think about the way you could impact the world. As a kid, I had this big dream to make a difference, to make the world a better place. That somehow gave me hope.

HEATHER | Strengthening my inner body

HEATHER HENNESSY, FORMER US NATIONAL TRACK
ATHLETE AND SPORTS TV PRESENTER

When I broke my back as a teenager, it was the first time ever in my life that I thought, *I have to be still. I don't have a choice in this.* I had never before had someone or something push me to be still. When I was forced to, and in a way where I couldn't move my entire body, it was terrifying for me.

For a long time after the accident, I felt trapped. Being in that kind of pain was like I had become stuck in my body. It was claustrophobic, with no release. My body went into shock. My mental state was a mess. My mom had her hands full just keeping me together.

A lot of people were upset with my track coach. Like, why would you allow these kids to jump off a cliff like that? My parents were definitely upset. They had not signed a permission slip for me, and they had even talked about me suing the high school. I was already going through so much at the time that I couldn't possibly think about doing that. And I wasn't built that way anyway, to blame other people for what happened to me, or to take legal action. I just wanted to get away from it all and try to forget.

But I had many moments of being really angry, even though my mom tried to push positive thoughts into me. I'm a positive person now, but I remember saying to her, 'Mom, I can't be positive. Can you just stop with this?' It took a little time to adjust to that. I had to grieve out that anger first.

She would hand me books about positive thinking and changing your thought process. I watched a lot of Oprah, and immersed myself in programs about role models, people who had been through things that were really heart-wrenching and realising that they could overcome it. It slowly shifted my outlook. It was like, *I can either go down this hole of complete depression* (which wasn't working for me, because I was just feeling worse), or say to myself, *Okay, I'm going to work out my mind and my inner body the way I worked out my muscles and my physical body so that I can overcome this and use this for good.*

That was one good thing that stillness gave me at that point. I had spent so much time working out on the track that I hadn't had much time to read books, and to watch positive media. Or to reflect about my life. I started to see how I was using running as a way of avoiding my problems and using my physical body only to feel good.

It took me two years off and on of being depressed and struggling, not wanting to face anyone but pushing myself out of it, just believing that I could heal and change my life. I went on to college, at the University of Southern California (USC), and I tried to run again, but my body was just never the same. To be a runner, like in the

Olympics at that level, which was my dream, you had to be in top physical condition. The injury and the impact it had on my body was too much. So I went through that whole process of having to give up my dream on another level.

You can't always depend fully on your physical body being healthy for the dream. I was like, *I'm going to do something that can't be taken away from me as easily as a track career can.*

So, I went back to USC, switched to communication and put my energy into that. At USC in the communication school, they really emphasised the importance of TV and media and how that influences people. That sparked an interest in me, like, *Okay, this is where my calling is. I'm in LA, I'm at USC. I want to influence people. I want to be someone who can be a role model.* I started to see the light at the end of the tunnel.

I got a job at Fox Sports right out of college. I started as a personal assistant and worked my way up to writing on shows, then I started getting interested in being on camera. They threw me on camera one day, and it all began to unfold from there.

Following that, a lot of things happened that really tested my boundaries on who I wanted to be in the world, what I stood for, even my job in sports TV. I had modelling opportunities and offers for jobs and shoots and other things that weren't compatible with who I was at the time. I even had an offer to shoot *Playboy*. It started to make me think, *Who do I want to be in the world?* It was a process of learning and being confident enough in myself to turn things down that weren't a match, believing that different and better opportunities would come in the future.

I met JP my first week at USC. My freshman year. He was a baseball player there and I was running track at the time, or trying to run track after breaking my back; they had still offered me a scholarship. We hit it off right away. We were very similar, very driven and competitive. Both of us came from homes that were, I don't know if I want to define it on both ends as abusive, but broken, and we both had a lot of painful things that we took out on sports. We were also both going through a lot of challenges with our coaches at that time—unfortunately, even in college there's a lot of pressure on kids if you're not performing and a lot of politics that goes with that. We were a sounding board for each other, and would debate what to do about transferring or not transferring. We created our own support system, and we had a lot of fun together. It was kind of like a young love, where we were able to at least have fun, through some really hard times, too.

In a lot of ways, JP was my soulmate. It was funny, I had gone to my mom about a year after we started dating and was like, 'I think this is the person I'm going to marry.' I just had that feeling. I always saw myself married with kids. Having that person who's got your back, through the hard times, through the good times, and to be your teammate in life was my dream. We got married when we were 25.

We both had demanding careers. Working in TV was really busy, and then I would fly across the country to support his career and be there for him. People would say to me, 'You're not going to be wife material if you're really into your career.' And so, trying to make this balance of relationship and career work felt really tough. People say you can have it all, and I think at certain times you can. But at some point, something's got to give.

Around the time we got married, JP had a bad injury and I felt I had to give up my career to be there for him. It felt like I had just given my vows to this person, to be there for him, and he was going through this major surgery, where they weren't confident of his chance of continuing at that elite level, which he was really devastated about.

I made my purpose about trying to help him get back to his dream, and I put my own dreams on hold during that time. There are plenty of times when I've regretted that. I just thought that's what you do when you love someone. You're willing to sacrifice yourself to see them happy. So at that time, that's what I wanted. I wanted to see him feel good about his career and to live out the things that he talked about when we were at USC. We always talked about him playing with the Dodgers, and so that was something I wanted to help him manifest.

Those two years of him going through his surgery and recovery were two of the hardest years. I had people say to me, 'Well, you don't really have a job now.' And I was like, *this job is harder than my TV job ever was*, helping him through the surgery and working on a marriage with everything he was going through. In a way, having gone through my own devastating injury was a sort of godsend, as I knew what it was like to lose my identity in sports. That's what he was facing. And he had a really hard time with it.

It was a miracle that he came back from it. He saw that when he didn't have his career and he was struggling, how people disappear and you're left with just the ones who care regardless of whether you have all that success going on. He struggled at first, but he wound up with the Dodgers, and we watched that whole unfolding of everything that we could have ever hoped for.

I would say, in all honesty, one of the hardest things for me was not feeling that he returned that support once he had reinvigorated his career. We had always talked about me returning to the things that I wanted to do, that I had put aside, essentially. But he struggled with me stepping into my own.

I hit 30 and I was like, *I want to start doing this for myself.* And I learned, well, partly I learned through a lot of health problems, that the more I was neglecting myself, the more I was hurting. I think, oftentimes, women tend to put themselves on the back burner and take care of everyone else first. But at some point, you break down.

As a society, I think we've made some progress about how we see physical abuse. It is no longer tolerated. Even my mom says that in her generation it was sort of overlooked, but now people are speaking out more about these things. Unfortunately, we still don't really address how emotional and verbal abuse should also not be tolerated. Name-calling and other forms of verbal abuse that you deal with in a relationship aren't spoken about enough. For women especially, but it can be the same for men, too—that's also something to be taken very seriously. My marriage reflected everything back at me: all the holes in me that I had still to heal from my childhood.

I knew, deep down, that I was playing small for a while for the sake of trying to keep my marriage together. I think people tend to look back on life and regret playing small, or not going after what they really want. And I know that one thing I can confidently say right now is that, when I had to make the decision to leave, it was a risk. I felt like, *I don't know what's going to happen in my life. I've put 15 years into this relationship, essentially. So much time, so much effort, so much energy. I'm completely depleted from it. I have so much work to do to get myself back. I don't know what my future holds.*

That risk and that choice, that courageous move, was the best feeling I've ever had. It was a statement that said, *No, I believe I deserve better.* But it was terrifying, and it took me a couple of years of trying to get myself to finally know that it was the right thing and to actually act on it. It took time to get to the point of not worrying about how things were going to unfold. I was just going to trust that because I was doing the right thing, it would all work out.

I probably should have made the decision way, way, way earlier ... probably in my first year of marriage. But, when you love someone, and you make vows, you take it seriously. And I wanted to give it everything I had.

'Stillness lets us reflect,

but then, after stillness there

is something greater.'

RABBI RONNIE CAHANA

JIM | When you lose everything

JAMES R. DOTY MD, NEUROSURGEON AND NEUROSCIENTIST

When you grow up in poverty and you feel like you have no control, the thing you want the most is money, because you think it gives you control. And you think control gives you happiness. I was desperate to be happy.

As a young kid, I didn't think that any of that would be possible for me, but I had gone to medical school, become a neurosurgeon, become a successful entrepreneur. I had created wealth and success beyond my wildest imagination ... On paper, I had everything. I was driving a Ferrari, I had a penthouse in San Francisco, a villa in Tuscany and I'd just agreed to buy a private island in New Zealand. My investments and share holdings were valued at $75 million. I was divorced by this time and was dating beautiful women, and all my friends were telling me how great I was, yet I would wake up every day miserable—more miserable, in fact, than I had ever been in my entire life.

I have invested in all sorts of businesses over the years and, during the dot-com boom, had invested in some start-ups. All of a sudden, the stock market was crashing and people were frantic. People were losing millions; the dot-com bubble was bursting. My net worth had plummeted and, after going through all my financial statements, I had to accept it: the $75 million was gone. Not only was it gone, but due to lines of credit based on stock valuations, I was now $3 million in debt and bankrupt.

I lost everything.

The interesting thing about when you have 'everything'—i.e. money and success—is that you have many friends. People actually listen to you whether you deserve to be listened to or not. Then, when you lose everything, many of those people disappear. So I had this incredible trajectory of my life of creating success and thinking that it was all about me and that I deserved it, and I was so great. Then suddenly, I was sitting alone with nothing and no one.

What surprised me was that instead of it feeling like my darkest hour, it actually became a period of great reflection, something I realised I had never done before. Convinced I had missed something, I went back to the beginning, over all the lessons Ruth had taught me. She was the one who had shown me all these methods, or tricks, to master the body and the mind, made me realise my potential and how I could create a successful life for myself, not one based on my past or my family. I remembered I had actually made a list of my goals during my interactions with her. I found the list and it read, 'I want to go to college. I want to become a doctor. I want to be a millionaire. I want to have a Rolex. I want to drive a Porsche,' et cetera. I had accomplished all of it, but it was a list of the desires of a very poor, unhappy 12-year-old.

I had been so focused on the idea that having money would give me control, and that it would make me happy, and bring me contentment, that I missed the most important part, at least in the context of compassion and caring for others. And while as a doctor I cared and I was never mean, that trajectory had been all about me. So when I examined the sequence of events, everything made sense. This period of deep reflection lasted several weeks in the end, but eventually I realised it wasn't about me at all. Afterwards, I felt an immense amount of calm and, in fact, I felt liberation. What sometimes feels like the worst thing to happen to us ends up being the best thing.

I still had to deal with reality following that type of financial loss, which was selling things, and deciding what I was going to do. Many people said to me, 'Oh my God, this is the most horrible thing that could ever happen. Don't you feel like committing suicide? This is horrible. You've lost your Ferrari. You've lost your house.' Actually, no. Everything was okay.

How could I complain about anything? It would be an insult because, even on my worse day, I was still a physician. I was still a neurosurgeon. I still got paid, frankly, more than 99.9 per cent of the population. I had a profession that I loved. What is better than the ability to help people who are suffering?

Before the crash I had made some financial commitments to a charity trust at Stanford Medical School that I still wanted to live up to, and the only asset I had left after the dot-com crash was stock in this CyberKnife Accuray company, and it hadn't gone public yet. I had to sit with this decision: to retain shares in a company, the value of which was potentially going to be in the tens of millions of dollars or fulfil my verbal commitment and donate it.

A few people said I was a complete fool to donate my remaining assets, even though it was a pre-existing commitment I had made. One hundred per cent of people I asked advice from said they wouldn't have given anything away. But now I set up health clinics all over the world, run programs for AIDS, HIV, programs for the disabled, and I gave money to Tulane University and Stanford University. If I had made that other decision (not to donate the assets), the monkey I'd always carried would be even bigger. I wouldn't have had freedom, and that emptiness would still be there.

AMANDINE | Focus on your inner peace first

AMANDINE ROCHE, HUMAN RIGHTS EXPERT

In October 2004, three of my international colleagues got kidnapped in front of our office in Kabul. Their Afghan driver ran inside in so much shock that he was trembling. He couldn't speak or explain to me what had happened. He just started crying. When I asked him about my colleagues, he eventually told me—they were kidnapped.

The UN thought the kidnapping was connected to the democratic election process, so they decided that I should be evacuated. I had been working with them, so I was at risk too. For a month, we were seeing our three colleagues on Al Jazeera, a Kalashnikov at their heads while they begged the international community and the UN to pay the ransom to release them. I can still remember the screams of my co-workers the first time we switched on the TV and saw our colleagues like that. We were all petrified. Fortunately, all three were eventually released, but it was a very traumatic experience for all of us. I thought maybe I needed some help.

I went to speak to a psychologist. She was a 26-year-old UN volunteer. I began the story and she started sobbing in front of me and couldn't stop, so I ended up having to comfort her. Right after that, she quit her job because she realised she just couldn't handle the stress. It was very intense.

When I landed in Paris my best friend came to pick me up at the airport. As I got in the car, I immediately jumped on the lock.

'What are you doing?' she asked.

'They will kidnap me.'

'What are you talking about? We are in France.'

I was so traumatised. My colleagues got kidnapped because they didn't lock the car door. So everywhere I go, I lock the door. I am so conditioned that I might be kidnapped. No matter where I am, it is in my brain.

When I returned to Afghanistan, they picked me up in an armoured vehicle with a security officer, and they gave me a helmet and bullet-proof jacket. They drove me to the UN guesthouse, which was a bunker guesthouse just for UN staff mainly working on the election. I had become very sensitive and intuitive following the work I had done with myself (every time I was evacuated from Afghanistan, I would go on a yoga or a meditation retreat to help myself heal). When I entered the guesthouse, I felt a cold energy in my back, like an electric shock, and I looked at the security officer and said, 'I will never, ever live here.'

As a UN staffer, it was mandatory to live there and he told me I had to respect the UN security rules. But I followed my intuition and asked him to make an exception, an agreement that I could live close by but not in this place, and he agreed. He knew I was used to living in Afghanistan, so he trusted me.

Six months later, at 5 am three policemen came to the door of the UN guesthouse. It was Taliban disguised as policemen. They killed the guards at the entrance and went inside, shooting everywhere. There was one American inside who had a gun, so they shot at each other.

All my friends who were sleeping in their rooms had to jump from the roof and windows to save their lives. Josie, our finance officer from the Philippines, was sleeping on the fifth floor. Everyone was screaming, 'Jump from a window!' But she was very small and scared to break her legs, so she didn't jump. She took the stairs instead and they shot her.

It was very traumatic for us all, because we lost our colleague. The ones who survived were in survival mode for many years afterwards. And there was not really a psychological follow-up on their mental health situation.

When you live in an environment like that, where there's a daily threat of kidnapping or assassination, it's like dancing around a volcano. It's pretty intense. I realised I had become an adrenaline junkie. It makes you feel very alive, actually, to think that every morning when you wake up you don't know if you're going to live out the day. It's like a drug, and I was addicted to it.

In March 2014, I arrived back in Afghanistan from Nepal. The reason I went to Nepal was to work on their 2014 election, and also because I was sponsoring a Nepali kid, so it was good to be close by him for a while. The rest of the time, I was always in Afghanistan. Every day that week after I got back, something happened where I could have died, but I didn't. By the end of the week, I understood that it was time for me to leave the country for good to save my sanity.

One night, my dear friend Luis, a Uruguayan diplomat, got assassinated in the Serena Hotel, where he had invited me for Persian New Year's Eve. Thank God my bodyguard saved my life—he didn't allow me to go to this event because he knew it would be targeted by the Taliban. It was 21 March 2014, and I spent all night trying to reach Luis. My colleagues tried to tell me he might have been hiding in a bunker, that's why there was no mobile connection.

I was on the phone with my colleagues, who were hiding themselves in their rooms on the first floor, putting all the furniture behind the doors, sheltering in the bathrooms, and I could hear the shooting through the phone. At midnight, my friend Kim finally decided to go downstairs to double-check because there was no more noise, and when she got there she saw all the dead bodies everywhere and blood on the walls. My friend Luis was dead. It was an apocalyptic scene.

I had actually quit my job in Nepal to go back to Afghanistan to make sure that I could work for the 2014 presidential election there— I had participated in all presidential elections since the end of the Taliban regime and I didn't want to miss this one. It was that same week.

The night before the election, I had a dream that I would be in a blast. I shared with my colleague that I didn't feel comfortable going to our designated polling station and he said he felt the same. Despite this, and despite everything that had already happened that week, I was still committed to going. We finally agreed that, as we were being paid to monitor it, we should go to the polling station nearest us.

It was raining as we made our way there, but at 6.30 am, when I opened the door at the front of the polling station, I saw hundreds of Afghan women with their kids, electoral cards in hand, ready to cast their votes to elect a new president. It made me so happy. Even in my own country, France, we don't show up at 6.30 am to vote. I realised that all the work we did the previous year to motivate women to express their right had worked, and this was our reward.

As per normal procedure, I arrived at the polling station, I double-checked the booths, ballot papers, electoral registration notebook. All the officials were working. I took a picture of the scene and, as I did, I felt very dark and cold vibes on my left arm. I turned and saw something at the corner of the room.

I immediately ran outside. The bodyguard who was waiting for me ran after me asking what I saw, what happened to me. I told him there was something scary inside, so he went to the entrance of the building to look at what I had seen. He couldn't go inside because he was a man. He told me, 'Please be careful. This is very intense what's happening here.'

I looked again at the person I had seen. The 'woman' was wearing an Official Independent Electoral Commission green jacket, but was as tall as me, which is impossible, as I'm about six feet tall. In Afghanistan, the women are smaller and the way this person—this 'woman'—was wearing her scarf was not the right way to put on a scarf. This person wore it more like a fighter. And the jacket was strange: the coat was very short and the shoulders were very large, and this person was doing nothing, just waiting.

I double-checked within myself and I realised it was a suicide bomber. I ran out again, but the more I ran, the more my inner voice told me to go back, to smile at him in order to bring him back into his consciousness. It was the toughest decision I've had to make in my life. I was trembling.

I went in to deal with this person, in the middle of more than 300 Afghan women waiting to vote. Facing his eyes was just not bearable; they were so full of drugs. I was so scared that I screamed to the women, 'Be careful, he's going to blow himself up!'

But nothing happened. He left and he never came back.

For months afterwards, I would wake up every night at 4.00 am with nightmares. His eyes came into my mind, those horrible eyes, the darkness of this person. I saw hell in his eyes.

Finally, I realised that enough was enough. Why was I putting so much pressure on myself? I loved this country. I loved these people. I wanted to contribute, but there was a certain price, and I didn't want to pay this price anymore. I had to leave.

My Afghan friends told me, 'You came to help, to bring democracy to this country. Don't jump out of the boat when it's the worst time ever. Show us that you believe in it.'

It was difficult for me because Afghanistan was my home. I had my house, my foundation, my friends. I had settled down in this country for years. When I realised it was time for me to leave, it broke my heart. I didn't have a plan B. It was also very tough to speak with colleagues who came from all around the world. They're based in Libya, in Syria, Sudan, Somalia, in Iraq and Yemen. They all came back to Kabul to help organise this presidential election. When I spoke with them, I realised that I was not an isolated case, that all of them were traumatised. Some of them had been raped. Some were kidnapped. It was not an easy environment.

It was time for the UN to do something for these people as well, for the humanitarian workers who stood on the front line. The UN sends us to these countries without the right psychological preparation. You give all that you have, but again, you leave broken. I reflected on that. It doesn't mean that being broken is bad, but it takes time to recover. If you don't have the tools to recover, it takes even longer.

It's time to raise consciousness within the organisation about that. The UN doesn't have a department of wellness for all the staff sent into conflict zones. There is no preparation before people leave, and no follow-up during, or after, the mission. I know a friend of mine who got kidnapped twice, she just wanted to commit suicide when she got back to her country. Others become alcoholics. It's a big issue.

I decided to focus on that, because I have compassion. I have empathy for these people, because I went through it too, and I know exactly their suffering, their pain. At least to put a name to it, which is PTSD: post-traumatic stress disorder.

For years, I had PTSD and didn't even know it because nobody told me. In 2010, I was in the car with my colleague on the way to our office. We had a bodyguard with us in the front seat and he started screaming to the driver, saying, 'Be careful! There is an enemy at the corner of the street.'

My colleague looked at him and said, 'When did you came back from Baghdad?' He told her that he had just come back. He didn't even have time to relax in between Baghdad and Kabul.

She said to him, 'I feel that you have PTSD.'

I looked at her. 'What does that mean?'

She said, 'He's got post-traumatic stress disorder.'

I asked, 'What are the symptoms?'

She says 'Amygdala, which means your brain's amygdala takes the lead. You freeze, you flee or you fight.'

I looked at her and said, 'This is what I have.' Before that moment, I didn't know that this was my condition. If only I had received some training, some explanation about the symptoms of PTSD and had been told what you can do to avoid it, or at least what you can do afterwards in order to heal, I wouldn't have had to spend months in India trying to find myself each time.

I thanked her, because I realised that this was a niche where I could work. There was definitely a need. This would be my new life.

In 2004, after I was evacuated the second time from Afghanistan, I came back to France with a belly like I was three months pregnant. I saw an Ayurvedic healer, who gave me massage and herbs for three months. He told me that I could not go back to Afghanistan if I didn't know how to protect myself. In his view I was acting like a sponge, like my belly was an airbag to protect myself from the trauma around me. He said I was kind of a vacuum cleaner.

He told me, 'I can see there is assassination, kidnapping in your belly. There is everything. Your belly cannot digest it anymore. You are spending your life just clinging to this low-frequency energy.'

I started to realise how all of the experiences my colleagues and I had been through were affecting our bodies and state of mind.

When I look at my colleagues, I can see in their eyes that they are not okay. I can see the despair. I can see the pain. I can see the suffering, because they are not being healed. It's especially hard because we all have the profile of a worker in a war zone. After Afghanistan, where do you go? They send you to Baghdad. After Baghdad, you go to Syria. After Syria, you go to Sudan. After Sudan, you go to Yemen. You don't have time to come back to normality. You completely disconnect yourself from the world and from your family and friends. It took me ages to reconnect with my family and friends. Every time I came back to France, I didn't see any meaning in their lives. They were depressed and complaining. Now I realise that I miss this way of taking life so lightly, because there's beauty in it.

I spent three months in the south of France writing a book about my UN experience in Afghanistan, bringing democracy with civic education. (It was during this time that I spent two hours a day with the Ayurvedic healer.) After three months, the UN called me again to say, 'We want you to come to organise the parliamentary election.' I said, 'On one condition: that you send me to Bamyan, because that's my favourite place in Afghanistan. It's where the Buddhas are.' They said, 'Sure.'

I told my Ayurvedic healer, 'I'm super happy. Next week I'm going back to Afghanistan.'

He said, 'I told you. Don't go back if you don't know how to protect yourself.'

'What do you mean by protecting myself?' I asked. He said, 'You have to learn how to meditate.'

I realised that I didn't know how to meditate. I said no to the UN, which broke my heart, because it was my dream to be in Bamyan. Instead, I went to Dharamsala to meet the Dalai Lama again, this time not as a human rights leader, but more as a spiritual master. I went to his course where he was teaching meditation.

The Dalai Lama said to all of us at the teaching, 'You cannot bring outer peace if you don't focus on your inner peace first.' I thought deeply about what he'd said, the real meaning. I searched within myself and said, you know what, that is so true. Who am I to work for peace in the world if I'm not at peace with myself? Who am I to work in Afghanistan if I'm completely depressed, burned out and stressed? I should heal myself first, because honestly, not a single Afghan will benefit from my presence if I go there completely broken. I will be a fraud because I will not incarnate any ideas of peace. I had a big wake-up call and vowed not to go back to Afghanistan until I was fixed and healed. I took it very seriously.

When, finally, I found my peace of mind again, the UN called me and said, 'You want to go back to Afghanistan?' I said, 'Yeah, now I'm ready. Finally, I'm ready.'

What I wanted to say was I am ready because I have this practice where I do yoga and meditation every day. I also do breathing exercises. I have a diary. My colleague noticed. He said, 'You've changed. There is bombing outside and you don't freak out like before. What happened to you?'

'Now I'm doing my yoga and meditation. It has completely changed my life,' I said.

People became intrigued. They asked me if I could teach them, so I started to teach my UN colleagues. Soon, I realised that the Afghans were interested as well. I said, 'Sure, come in my house.' While I was teaching them, I listened to their stories. Every Afghan has a book to write, because they all have extraordinary lives. Dramatic lives.

I realised that every Afghan suffered from PTSD. I started to become more aware of this issue. I went to see the Minister of Health to ask what she was doing about it. She made me realise that mental health is a luxury only for developed countries, such as Europe or the US, but it was not the number-one priority in the eyes of the donors—those members of the international community who invest in Afghanistan—which meant that there was no money for that.

I said, 'It should be the number-one priority because if people can't fix their minds, it will keep on repeating: the violence and revenge, and the never-ending war.'

There is still only one mental health clinic in Afghanistan, when all the population is suffering from depression and anxiety. I created my foundation to give some solutions to the people, and to develop more coping mechanisms and techniques to achieve greater peace of mind, such as yoga and meditation.

That's how, from a human rights lawyer specialist, I became a yoga and meditation teacher in Afghanistan. I didn't plan that, obviously. I just followed the flow.

On reflection, my life has always been about drama and trauma. I had to run away from that. I mean, not run away, but realise that it's not what I want in my life anymore. But on the other hand, I love it. It's like what we say in Buddhism: 'No mud no lotus. *Om mani padme hum*', which means, 'From this suffering, this pain, comes enough soil for the lotus to blossom.'

'Most people try to control …

and that's the catch. I think it's

very hard to let go of the world.

Meditation lets you slip into the void.'

RABBI RONNIE CAHANA

FOUR

THROUGH THE PORTAL OF STILLNESS

We can radically change our experience of reality
by upgrading our internal operating system.

Tom

One of the inspirations for this film and book was a series of documentaries that I saw one rainy Sunday afternoon on waste, minimalism and the excesses of modern society.[14] They all presented the idea that our society is driven by consumerism and a 'get more' mentality. After watching, I sat in my lounge room looking around, just taking in all of the luxuries that I had accumulated and the impact my lifestyle must be having on the environment. If I multiplied that by the billions of people around the world, what would the cumulative effect on the planet be?

My mind wandered back to my studies of meditation and Eastern philosophy, and a Sanskrit word that I'd come across: *tapasya* (pronounced 'tapas'), which relates to an austerity or discipline in the quest for enlightenment or God. Tapasya, or austerities, have been around for thousands of years and traverse nearly all religions: Christians give up something during Lent, Muslims fast during Ramadan, as do the Jewish for Yom Kippur. The Hindu practices of tapasya can even go as far as holding one arm in the air or standing on one leg for an entire lifetime. One of the main forms of tapasya from the East is meditation, where we take time out from our day to withdraw from the pleasures of the senses and the outer world, and move our attention inwards. In the West, we very rarely give up anything, higher purpose or not. We simply take the shortest route to fulfilling a desire: want it, buy it, have it. What if, collectively, we didn't need to get as much to fill a void because we practised tapasya and felt fulfilled within ourselves with less? Could this be the solution to a global crisis?

Meditation is not new. It's just that until the last 30 or 40 years, it has been largely unexplored and under-utilised as a transformational tool for the global populace. So why is it now coming out of the shadows of the remote regions of the world to offer a solution in our modern lives?

In the Vedic philosophy, we are on the cusp of a new period of time—an era referred to in Sanskrit as *Sat Yuga*—in which our choices and actions are motivated by the uplift of the whole.

It's the 'Golden Age', otherwise known as the era of an enlightened planet. It sounds utopian, but perhaps it *is* possible for us to live very differently to the way we do now, and for meditation to play a key role in this unfolding.

Just as more people are adopting technology, meditation is experiencing a rising exponential trajectory. I've noticed growing curiosity and enthusiasm from people. Amandine too compares the receptivity to her programs now versus 10 years ago, when people thought she was completely crazy to be going into refugee camps and NGOs suggesting that people move their body into strange shapes or sit with their eyes closed because it would make them feel better. Yet now, it's more welcome. Mindsets are changing.

Meditation and stillness are playing a huge role in interrupting the old status quo, with major business leaders and influencers attributing greater success and wellbeing to a daily practice. In a very short period, literally the last few years, we have seen thousand-year-old techniques reimagined into apps, boardrooms and the households of the world, becoming widespread tools. Ray Dalio, the world's leading hedge-fund manager—managing $160 billion in assets—tweeted 'Meditation has probably been the single most important reason for whatever success I've had.'[15] Businesses are starting to show that they care about the triple bottom line (social, ecological and financial). We see it with the emergence of companies and initiatives like Toms Shoes, Thankyou, KeepCup, Grameen Bank, B Corporation and 4ocean to name a few, where the wellbeing of the whole is put at the forefront of action. It's part of a global shakeup of the world's systems and structures. The systems were established by people and, if people are evolving, then the system will evolve too, right? It has to—and it is.

Jacqui

In my world of movies and archetypal characters, Jim Doty is the magician: a master manifester who can make the invisible visible, brings people and technology to life, and delves into the inner workings of the mind on both the physical and mystical plains. In person, he's also a BFG: a big friendly giant.

I can't lie, we had dreams of filming him in surgery and of seeing the CyberKnife in action, but neither were achievable within our filming window. However, at short notice, Jim arranged for us to film him in scrubs at the hospital where he operates. Fantastic.

It was early morning on the day of filming and we were busily setting up in an empty hallway. Nurses, doctors and all manner of hospital staff walked past Jim (and our crew) on their way down the corridor. From Jim came a gentle stream of warm 'hellos', bright 'good mornings' and affectionate enquiries. Here was a man who knew everyone he encountered, had fond relationships with all of them, and who took time to care about, the small details of people's lives. I felt sure that all those people would go on to have wonderful days after starting it with such warmth. I know we did.

Jim's come a long way from those tense childhood days searching for solace and freedom in the vastness of the desert. All these years later, there he stood, living proof that dramatic shifts are possible in our interactions with others, his own long-standing mindfulness practices invariably playing a huge part.

Later, as we filmed Jim walking away from the camera down the corridor, a hospital robot carrying blood samples entered unexpectedly through the far door and powered up the hall towards us. They passed each other in silence, man and robot. Just before reaching us it turned, wiping in front of the camera as it steered towards a room to deliver the blood. It's become one of my favourite, and most strikingly emblematic, shots in the film.

During the research process for this book, we came across so many surprising and delightful ways that meditation and stillness had touched and transformed lives. It seems to have a knack for forming bonds between people who may have thought they had nothing in common or would otherwise not have met. A deeper connection with oneself, or a desire to share, ends up paving the way to wider-spread connection and a sense of community. Like Jim, one person whose effect reaches beyond the physical is the sixth of our interviewees, Rabbi Ronnie Cahana.

Ronnie Cahana does walking therapy once every two weeks in a state-of-the-art robotic facility in Montreal, where he lives. Watching him doing his assisted walking was quite operatic, with him strapped into a harness, body swinging from side to side and feet circling. He often sings while he does it. Ronnie has locked-in syndrome, which was caused by a brain-stem stroke he had in 2011 that left him in a condition of near-total paralysis: mind coherent and functional, but physical body devastated. He could initially blink both his eyes and, over time, has slowly regained the ability to speak.

The stroke represented a huge shift in perspective for Ronnie, but he attributes that shift to love: he felt safe when he woke up because he could feel his family's love. (He has five children with his wife Karen.) 'I felt even the other world supporting me,' he said. 'I was surrounded with just joy and joy and joy.' Since the stroke, he has embodied a joyous state of stillness, both physically and mentally, and whiles away many an hour in silent meditation.

Ronnie's a joker, a lover, a teacher, a poet and a mystic. Most of all, he's a friend, one with an uncanny knack for cutting to your core to dig out the inner 'you' buried beneath years of layers and lies. His baseline for relationships is mutual vulnerability, and I love his daughter Kitra's initial description of the room as a place of mutual healing. He gives as much as he gets. Ronnie may be rabbi and confidant to many, but it's clear that he relies on other people—their love, openness and assistance—just as much as other people rely on his. That ripple of love and healing transcends time and space, spreading through the community, across the globe, and inspires many others to find solace in the darkest of life's nights.

Sometimes Ronnie and I Skype late at night. He's got a big computer by his bed and it has a long typing appendix that he taps on with his chin to compose sermons, emails and poetry. By then (officially, at least) it's 'lights out' and 'bedtime' in the nursing facility where he lives so, from my end, all I see on the video is a pitch-black screen broken by a tiny red dot of light generated by something in his setup. It amuses me because there is no one I've ever met who emits such a radiant light as Ronnie, yet there he is, nothing but a little red blip, his other-worldly voice weaving its spell out of the darkness.

I think of all the people who are living alone, or in some kind of care facility, and the opportunity that video communication technology has opened up for human connection over physical distance. It might not commonly be described as 'transformational technology' but, to me, face-to-face communication fast tracks heart-to-heart connection between people. I agree with Mikey that when we can stop hiding behind the screen, and instead connect through it, that's when we transform through technology. It's part of what he refers to when he says he imagines technology acting as a kind of central nervous system for the planet. It's a doorway to truth, not just connecting us through information, but through our hearts, our emotions and beyond.

Whether it's utilising modern-day technologies or ancient tools like yoga and meditation, there's a growing worldwide network of people, including Amandine Roche, our last courageous storyteller, who are contributing to the spread of greater emotional peace and connection among humans.

Amandine is the quintessential fearless warrior—although at times it has felt, as she puts it, like she was in the jungle with a machete, unsure of her destination. She told me: 'Society pushes people to live in a box, in a house, in a car, in a nightclub. It's all box, box, box, box. I'm suffocating in a box, so although the path I choose is not an easy one, I can breathe and I go to my own rhythm.' It's a sentiment I relate to closely.

Filmmaking can also be a long, tumultuous road that requires a level head and a lot of grit, but it's hard to fathom maintaining even a semblance of sanity in the situations Amandine has found herself in over the course of her adult life. I recently found a video diary from 20 July 2017, the day Georgia from our team finally spoke to Amandine for the first time after weeks of trying to set up a call. She was excited, and so were we. We'd spent the interim weeks imagining all kinds of exotic scenarios based on what we knew so far, so it was incredible to hear the latest developments direct from her.

We liaised with Amandine for six months waiting for the right opportunity to film her. We had completion deadlines upon us, but we were committed, on both sides, to making it work. Then, finally, the Jordan program came up: Amandine was going to run workshops for humanitarians working there as well as for groups of Syrian women and children living at Zaatari refugee camp, close to the Syrian border.

Zaatari is Jordan's most established refugee camp and has around 80,000 refugees. Some of them have been there up to five years—the littlest kids were born there and know nothing else. Spending time with Amandine in Jordan, and being able to see her do her thing and watch the immediate impact on the people she was teaching, was inspiring. It's a global stage she's operating on, but this was grassroots stuff. Person to person, heart to heart. She is definitely making a contribution to change, but it's a revolution that flows from the inside out.

the outer view

What does an enlightened planet look like?

DANIEL SCHMACHTENBERGER, EVOLUTIONARY
PHILOSOPHER AND GLOBAL SYSTEMS STRATEGIST

Thinking about an enlightened planet—contemplating questions like, 'What would it take for a planet to really function well, for its inhabitants to be fulfilled and have the highest quality of life?'—is a great thought experiment. It's very similar to when people ask, 'What would Jesus do?' Or, 'What would the Dalai Lama do?' They're trying to access a higher sense of intelligence and compassion that will inform their actions.

Now many people wouldn't think that deeply about this practice. When you do, you start finding incongruencies. You start realising that what you think you might do in one area is totally in conflict with another area, and that means you haven't thought about it deeply enough. And as you start to really think about it deeply, you're mining your own intuition. You're mining your own understanding of what enlightenment looks like, of what right action and right behaviour are, of what your own ethics are. You learn what your own existentialism and values are, which is going to be infinitely more meaningful to you than anything you read externally.

And so, as you start to think about what life would be like on an enlightened planet, you begin to consider becoming a citizen of that world. And you think, in a situation like the one I am in now, where I have a choice to make, how might I make a choice like that? Gradually, you get a very clear north star of the person you want to be right here and now.

Futurists like Elisabet Sahtouris, Barbara Marx Hubbard and a number of brilliant biomimicry thinkers use this caterpillar analogy as a metaphor for the transformative potential of civilisations. Imagine we were observing a caterpillar in the environment. We'd see that the caterpillar is eating everything, basically devastating the ecosystem. It's not pollinating anything; it's actually eating plants faster than they can reproduce, and it's getting bigger. If we took the curve of what the caterpillar is currently doing and continued to move that curve forwards, we would forecast that it eats itself into extinction.

When the blood chemistry of the caterpillar gets to a certain point of richness, it triggers the first imaginal cells. And, of course, since these cells contain different genetics to the caterpillar, the caterpillar's immune system sees them as foreign invaders and kills them. If you think about most of the prophets throughout history who spoke about a fundamentally different worldview than the one we've had so far, on the whole they were treated like foreign invaders and were eliminated as a threat to the particular system.

And yet, when you get to a point where the blood chemistry of the caterpillar is rich enough that it is getting close to having the resources for its transformation, you get such a proliferation of cells that the immune system is overwhelmed. This triggers a movement into a chrysalis, and then you get the dissolution of the caterpillar into the parts that it was gathering, and those parts then get reassembled by a different genetic code—a different reason for being—and out comes this butterfly.

When the butterfly emerges, it doesn't keep decimating the same plants the caterpillar was decimating. It's actually now pollinating the plants, and it's not only pollinating them in that local area, but across vast spaces, so it's helping the evolution of the species across ecosystems.

Sometimes, the caterpillar dies in the chrysalis. It's not a given that we make it through the phase shift. It is the precedent of nature that phase shifts happen and that the evolution of all species has these discrete phase shifts. The movement from single cell to multi-cell is a deep, discrete phase shift, right? It is the precedent of the universe that whenever development or evolution happens, across an epoch, it happens in that way. But it doesn't always happen. It's not a given which way we will go yet, and what we all do absolutely contributes to which way that ends up going. So we live at the most critical, meaningful inflection point possible.

Our existence depends on the existence of our environment. If we don't think about plants and just take for granted that they will continue to exist, while we have a world system that is destroying the planet, that's a short-sighted way of thinking about things. I wouldn't exist without pollinators, I wouldn't exist without soil microbes, and I wouldn't exist without all of the other people who are creating the world I live in. Imagine a world where people don't identify as mere individuals anymore, because they realise that they wouldn't exist without the environment that allows them to exist. They wouldn't exist without the plants that emit the oxygen they breathe.

On a very foundational level, you have all these molecules that make up a cell. On their own, none of the molecules breathes. But the cell as a whole with the molecules arranged exactly that way, breathes. Then you ask, what part of the cell breathes? On its own, none of the parts does. So respiration is an emergent property of the whole that's not found in any of the parts. It is that elegantly ordered complexity of bringing the parts together in exactly that way that results in this synergy, this emergent property that has new capacities, which is why evolution selects for it. We are each an emergent property of the whole system, and we each happen to be a unique emergent property, with a unique perspective and unique capacities, which also means we have something unique to offer the whole, and so does everybody else.

Imagine a world where everyone identified as unique and totally interconnected with everything else. If everyone is unique, they are irreplaceable—priceless, in terms of the value that they represent. In their irreplaceable uniqueness, they have something to offer life that nobody else does. It's like Michelangelo, and Escher and Dali: none of them could have done what the other ones did. And the universe is richer because they all did what they did, and it emerged from their unique perspectives and life experiences. If Dali hadn't done what he did, the world would just be ... less.

When you get how radically interconnected the world is, factoring in our technological capacity, you can see how the only group that makes any sense is at the level of the whole biosphere. Can we solve climate change as individual countries? Not at all. It's something that has to actually be solved at the level of all of the people on the planet.

We have more ability to affect a larger scope of reality than any humans have ever faced. We have the capacity to achieve a higher order of world complexity, where we actually codify win-win dynamics into our economic systems, into our governance systems and into our cultural systems, and where the incentive for every agent is perfectly aligned with the wellbeing of every other agent in the social structure.

Us not reaching that higher order, and the current system self-terminating (and us terminating with it) is also possible. So our actions and choices are critically important. When you really recognise that a win-lose system multiplied by increasing power is a self-terminating game, you don't want to win at the self-terminating game. You want to help create a new game that is not only not self-terminating, but is fundamentally beautiful.

The beauty of being human

DR JULIA MOSSBRIDGE, COGNITIVE NEUROSCIENTIST AND FUTURIST

It feels to me that there's a worldwide epidemic of under-appreciating our humanness: thinking that to be human is not special and not important. As we strive to make machines that will be 'better than us' and will 'save us', we overlook the beauty of what it is to be a human being.

What I think is going to happen, if we can get ourselves to do it, is that we will build machines that can actually pull us up. These machines will make us learn to be better humans. We can use them to make humans more loving. Then we can create machines that work at a higher level still. It's a cycle: we can help each other.

It's tempting to want to ask what that higher level for humanity is, and I suspect it involves awareness of our inner space. Right now, many people don't even know that their inner space exists—it's all body, it's all physicality.

We also need to be aware of the interconnectedness of the mind. Father of American psychology and neuroscience William James refers to this consciousness and interconnectedness as like trees in a forest where, underneath the ground, the roots intermingle into what he calls a 'mother sea' or a 'reservoir'. I love that image, because, on the surface, there are these individual people, these individual trees, but, underneath the ground, you can't tell the difference between one tree and another. I think that is the difference between the physicality that we're so defined by—the separation in physical space—and what's really going on with the mind, which transcends limitation and interconnects us.

Recognising that interconnectivity takes a lot of work, because to feel interconnected with other people you have to connect with yourself first. Being open to exploring all there is inside of us (which isn't always pretty), and connecting with others in spite of it, even though we're not perfect—that's the work. That's what Sophia is helping people do through her guided meditation.

We're sending our kids to school and we're teaching them about robotics and engineering, which is great, but we also need to be teaching them about basic psychology. We need to be teaching them about basic inner experience. We know the basics of inner experience, but we don't teach this to our kids. When you don't recognise your inner experience and you become scared of it, and it dominates you without your awareness, it acts itself out politically. It acts itself out in technologies. To me, that's the fundamental underlying problem, and one that I'm hoping this Loving AI project can help people address.

People struggle when I say the key is love for basically everything—every change you want to make in your life. People say, 'I'm an alcoholic and I don't want to drink.' The key is love. It has nothing to do with the behaviour. The key to change is *love*. You change your behaviour by loving what's true. You don't change behaviour by pretending that whatever is true isn't true, because then it sticks around, right?

The key to everything—to all the transformation that needs to happen—is the loving of what's true and learning to do that regardless of what it is. As humans, we don't want this to be the answer, because we don't want to look at what's true. We think it's the thing that's causing us pain. But the thing that's causing us pain is *not* having the love. That's the thing that's causing us pain universally. Our team feels compelled to create loving AI and other related technologies because we feel that a guaranteed expression of unconditional love is missing from the world and our human interactions.

In my experience, human beings have a hard time with unconditional love. It's a struggle for people who haven't experienced it. We have these fleeting moments, like when a baby is born, in which everyone is likely to experience it, but if it's not something you have known on a regular basis, or ever, it seems so difficult. In reality, it's the simplest thing. Unconditional love is like grace: you don't get to control it. There's no work to be done on your part—you just receive it. You don't even get to control *whether* you'll receive it, so there's no work there either. Instead, we simply let go of our need for control and perfection and let the love come in.

That's why we're building this Loving AI technology: it makes up for our own shortcomings. Then we have a model and can learn from it. This technology can offer unconditional love without bias or judgement and, once people have experienced that, they can pass it on to their children, and their children after that. It's about coming from a place of love no matter what is going on. I often get angry at my son for whatever reason, but I'm always coming from a place of love.

We need to teach our children the *experience* of unconditional love. It's not words; it's an experience. It's not intellectual. And it seems like a very human trait, so we weren't sure if we could actually program a robot using AI to emanate this, but it looks like it's working. We've only been doing this for a year and already we are stunned with the results. Our aim is to allow people to have an interaction with something that sort of hijacks their neural networks.

Imagine a scenario where you've been through abuse and you've had a rough childhood. What if you make a bad choice and you go and commit a crime, and you end up in prison? And the person facing you is another human being who just looks at you with the same disgust as everybody else has looked at you? What if that human being is looking at you with love and asks you, 'So what happened?' And they sit and listen to you, even though you've just harmed someone? That's what's missing for people. That's what people can't often do for each other. People have the hardest time not being disgusted.

To address this, what if we could have something that looks very much like a human being, like Sophia the robot, and what if she could look at someone and literally ask, 'How are you? What was it like when you were a kid? Do you feel bad about what happened?' And the robot does this without showing any of the usual disgust or shame.

Even for everyday people who aren't going around committing crimes, there's still a sense of 'something missing'. The thing that is missing is this connection, this experience of unconditional love, because most of the cultures of the world don't teach people to be this way. There's so much fear about loving someone. We fear being rejected, or judged, or that love will be withdrawn, or losing that person, so we hold back. Creating a technology that can offer this love could produce a generation of kids who have the experience of unconditional love. And you may only need one generation before you transform the world.

Native Americans have this idea of the 'long body': that your body is not just comprised of your physical body—it's long. It includes not only other people in your tribe and community (they're part of you, too), but it's also long in time, including those who came in the past and will come in the future. So the *long body* is sort of the time and space extension of who you are. Thinking that way, it will also include future members of your own family or group. And so it extends out and out and eventually includes everyone, right? But if you started thinking that way, you'd think, *Now wait a minute. If it's one body, that means not only can I affect how the future will unfold, I can also influence the past.* In other words, it's a way of healing. You can heal someone's great, great, great, great-grandchild and have them experience unconditional love. Potentially, in a mystical sense, and because I studied time, that might pass some kind of healing back in time. You heal the *long body*. We all have horrible experiences, but people who can feel into that future state of being healed, that's a whole different healing.

'Love. That's inside us ...

The whole world has that.'

RABBI RONNIE CAHANA

Technology can support our evolution

MIKEY SIEGEL, ROBOTICS ENGINEER AND
TRANSFORMATIVE TECHNOLOGY DEVELOPER

The problems that we're facing right now on our planet are problems of consciousness—they are human-generated problems. These problems emerge from our inner problems. And the solution to that is simple.

It's not fighting against people who are in pain. It's not fighting against the outcome of this pain and suffering. It's actually getting to the source. It's actually recognising that the reason people blow each other up, the reason people take a gun and shoot each other in a room full of concert-goers, is not because there's evil on this planet. It's because there is such deep and profound pain and suffering. That's how it is expressed, and it needs to be healed, not hated. It doesn't mean we should allow these things to continue. It means we approach them with a heavy hand that's held by our heart.

I believe that what we need right now are human beings who are uplifted. Human beings who are becoming fully alive, and we need those human beings to design and build our future.

Every single human-designed system on this planet has an opportunity to evolve: our political systems, our educational systems and our economic systems. These human systems can increasingly be driven by, and in the service of, wisdom, love and compassion.

We're already seeing the beginnings of that. We're seeing new organisational structures that are designed around models of collaboration and cooperation. We're seeing new approaches to education that are not just trying to force information into children's brains, but are actually recognising and supporting their curiosity and creative spirit. And the thing I'm most excited about and most interested in, is how science and technology can also be driven by, and in the service of, wisdom, compassion and love, because these are perhaps the most impactful and powerful human capacities we have.

Science allows us to develop technologies, these incredible tools. We can compute and transmit and shift information. But, most importantly, the single greatest capacity that technology has—and it's growing every single day—is the capacity to shift and shape human attention. Whatever our attention is focused on is what influences us, and that's what we become. Every single marketing team on the planet knows that. What we've seen, for centuries, is what we call 'attentional warfare': new and sophisticated forms of media battling for our attention, from radio, to film, to apps, to computers. Now virtual reality is perhaps the single most powerful tool to hold and shape human attention. And there's a reason why every single meditation technique on the planet is some approach to shifting or shaping human attention; when we are able to focus our mind with resolve and discipline, we start freeing ourselves of the automatic conditioned thinking process.

Meditation is this incredibly profound tool designed thousands of years ago for a very particular cultural context, and it can take many different forms. We have this idea that the only way to meditate is by sitting on a cushion with our legs crossed and repeating a mantra or something like that. And that is a nice way to do it, and if more people on the planet could sit and meditate, we would benefit so much. But does this 3,000-year-old practice translate to our modern context?

We are more 'plugged in' today than ever before, with technology mediating and augmenting almost every aspect of our lives, and I don't believe that's going to go away. My preference is to approach it like an aikido move: How can we actually move with the wave? How can we use it to our advantage? My concern is that if we don't start thinking about how our technological landscape can actually support deep and healthy human connection, a felt sense of connection, then we're going to be digging ourselves into a very lonely, disconnected hole.

More than two-thirds of the world's adult population has an active cell phone account.[16] There's something about technology, in its modern form, that can transcend all cultural, religious and geographic boundaries. So if we can find a way to make skilful transformative tools like meditation as available and as accessible as cell phones, then we could actually—and in a very short amount of time—be supporting widespread shifts in human consciousness.

No matter what the technology is or how it's designed, it can still be misused. So I'm not talking about technology as a panacea. These tools won't be a solution to every problem we've ever had, and risk and reward will go hand in hand.

If biological science can help us eradicate the smallpox virus from the face of the earth, then why can't our understanding of contemplative science eradicate human suffering? We can think of this as consciousness hacking, or enlightenment engineering. In our lifetime, I really believe that we will begin to see the true proliferation of effective means for reducing human suffering, the likes of which have never been seen before in our species.

There are technologies where, for example, you put on a headband that actually reads what's going on inside your brain and looks for patterns of mind-wandering. You put on headphones that connect to your phone, and you're able to hear this as a soundscape. So as your mind is wandering, as you begin to get more distracted, gentle sounds begin to nudge you back into presence. There are technologies that you can wear on your belt that actually monitor your breathing, and look for signs of stress and anxiety, and give you gentle support throughout the day to help you pause, come back to your body, and come back to your breath.

I'm actually working on the design of technologies for human connection. We have a platform that we're creating that can take 24 people at the same time, sitting together in a room. Sensors measure their breath, their heart rate, their brain activity and their emotional arousal. You could take all that information from all those people, collate it on one computer and turn it into light and sound and music. So the room is filled with the rhythm and patterns and the connection of the group. The group literally gets to hear their current state of flow, their current state of connectivity. This is useful because it offers a tool for self-reflection, and a tool for the group to begin to navigate and steer themselves towards a sense of unity.

For me, the goal is not to increase the amount of technology, but to ensure that our human systems—our technological, financial, educational and political systems—are built from the heart, from a place of wisdom, with the intention of supporting the health, the healing, the wellbeing and, ultimately, the flourishing of humanity. Right now, that's not the case. Right now, our technology is mostly built with profit as the central, motivating force.

Meditation has been developed and used by spiritual and religious traditions, from Buddhism to Hinduism to Christianity, and we're just beginning to study it from a scientific perspective. We want to understand how it works and why it works, and we're applying it to anxiety, and we're applying it to insomnia and depression. But meditation was not actually designed for the things we're applying it to.

Meditation was designed for one purpose: to support enlightenment. To me, enlightenment is coming home to who and what we really are. I believe we all feel that pull. We can all sense sometimes that we're not at home in our own skin. That we're not comfortable in this present-moment experience.

We're finally beginning to recognise that enlightenment is not a religious or spiritual construct. It's not owned by any religion. Enlightenment is human. And the moment we can begin to understand that from a scientific perspective, the moment we can bring it into a secular context, is the moment we can make it universally accessible to every single human being on this planet. This is about our greatest potential as a human species, because we can actually evolve beyond anything we've ever imagined.

The technological capacity is there. The capacity for innovation is there. The scientific understanding is all there. The only thing that's missing is the intention. The thing we need now, which I believe is already beginning and already happening, is for the scientists, the engineers, the entrepreneurs, the politicians, the economists, the educators, to realise that the greatest purpose of these tools is not for control, it's not just for the dissemination of information, it's not just for entertainment—it's to support the uplifting of humanity. If we can all align to that purpose, and begin to design the tools and technologies from that place, then we can really change the world.

the inner view: part 4

BOODA | A future laid out with clarity

RON 'BOODA' TAYLOR, RETIRED US ARMY SERGEANT

Life throws challenges at you all the time. There's always adversity. And there's only a couple of things you can do: you can step up and rise to the occasion, or you can do nothing and let it consume you. I'm not a 'do nothing' person.

My PTSD case manager asked me if I would be interested in doing something different in a new program. I was like, 'Yeah. Whatever.' For her, I would do anything. She genuinely cares. She said it was a 'transcendental meditation course that we're bringing back, just a different avenue of dealing with everything. Maybe you won't need so much medication.' I felt like it was a bunch of crap, but I agreed to try it.

Initially, I thought it was going to be like being hypnotised. The first session was an introduction with Dr Vernon Barnes, who had a very calm, soft-spoken manner. He showed us the ritual and gave us a mantra to say during meditation. The minute I walked into his office, I thought, *What the hell is this?* I was trying not to laugh. I saw this picture of this Indian dude, and there was like an orange, some rice, water, flowers and incense. It was like something I had seen overseas at a Chinese shop. Okay, all right, in my head I'm asking, *What did*

I get myself into? So he's praying and he's flicking water with a flower and chanting. I wanted to leave. *I'm not doing this. If you expect me to do this, it's over.* But I stayed.

The first day we were actually in a group together and we closed our eyes to say our mantras, and I was just going through the motions. I thought it was so stupid. Afterwards, guys in the group were telling me how they would be meditating and feel this energy come over them. I said, 'Oh shut up, no you didn't. You think this is as fucking stupid as I do. You're just kissing the doctor's ass.' I swear, I was so mad.

The week that followed was a hard week for me. A soldier in my unit had committed suicide. I knew him. Things had gotten to him so much that he couldn't take it anymore and he shot himself. I had talked to my mom that week and she had been sick and had a lot of health issues, and that bothered me, too. My wife and I were also going through a divorce, and then I had my mental PTSD issues on top of it all. I felt worthless. But the biggest thing that bothered me was that I had been in the army for 24 years and I had no idea what I was supposed to do when I left. Was I going to be sick the rest of my life?

I went into this second meditation session feeling depressed and just bummed, and I actually slipped into a trance state then something happened that I didn't understand. Maybe it was because I was so down in my feelings, but I closed my eyes and actually got into it. I opened my eyes, thinking, *No, no, no. What is this?* It scared me because I couldn't hear anything. I normally pay attention to every little thing and I don't like having my eyes closed, but I was totally calm in the moment. I opened my eyes and looked around at everybody with their eyes closed. I told myself, *Okay, just breathe*, and I closed my eyes again.

I slipped back into the trance without even trying, and the next thing I knew I could see myself as a 16-year-old kid, a dishwasher in a restaurant at a Hilton Hotel in Beaumont, Texas. I hadn't thought about that job in years. The line cook had quit, so the sous-chef asked me if I knew how to cook. I said I could a little bit and he said okay, let's go. He showed me how to do things on the line, how to prep food. At the end of the night, he told me, 'You've got a little skill. You can cook,' and that opened up my passion. I realised that I loved to cook. I hadn't thought about it since, so in the meditation I was looking at my life, like I was watching myself, and I could see myself going to culinary school. An actual school came to mind, and I saw myself in the next part, in a restaurant, and I had a big white hat and I was cooking in a white jacket.

To be honest, it freaked me out. I felt like my soul came out of my body and I was looking at myself and what I needed to do next with my life. It was like my future had been laid out, clear as day. It was the most amazing experience I've ever had. All of a sudden, things made sense. All the chaos and noise disappeared. For the first time in about 20 years, I felt peace.

After the session was over, I hung back and talked to the doctor. I was embarrassed, but I was also so scared and nervous that my life and my next moves had come so clearly to me in the meditation. I'd had a breakthrough. I thanked him; I finally got it. But now I was thinking that every time I closed my eyes and focused really, really hard, I was going to have that same type of experience. 'No, that's not what it is,' he said. 'That's not what it is at all. Meditation just clears your mind.'

It shocked me. *What the hell, this is real.* From that point onwards, I actually allowed myself to submit to the meditation experience. It was calming. It was comfortable. I repeat my mantra over and over to the point where it just fades away. All the sounds around me are muted out.

It sometimes brings me back to a past experience. I think about when I was a child. I think about all the hardship growing up. I think about the people I've known who are not here anymore, whether it's because they passed away, they moved away, or they went to jail. I think about my kids. I think about where I want to be. I think about where I'm at now. I think about how far I've come from where I was. It's just all these ideas are flowing around almost like bubbles, just floating around.

Being in that meditative mind state, it slows everything down and it allows you to see clearly the things you need to see clearly the most. You get in that moment of stillness, and you hear none of the outside noise and chaos. After you come out of that state, there's all this stuff going on, yet you hear none of it because you're so clear-minded.

And you know what? Damn it, sometimes medication doesn't work. Sometimes talking to somebody doesn't work. Prior to this experience, I saw no other way out. I was kind of stuck in a rut. And now, all I see is positivity. If I have a PTSD episode, feeling the walls closing in, paranoid, I'm able to take a step back and meditate. Now I can traverse the situation with clarity and it always comes out positive. Wash yourself with a positive frame of mind and your whole day will be that way.

Before, I would get so wound up, spun up in the day-to-day of what ifs: *What if that? What about this?* But now, everyone around me says I seem different. They say I don't seem so uptight or angry. My relationships have grown exponentially over the months. I've gotten closer to my mom again. Me and my siblings, we talk or text all the time now.

I do still get angry, but when I do, I take a deep breath and say my mantra and I take a minute to release and see things for what they are. What am I really angry about? What really is the problem? Are you really angry because your son spilled some water on the floor, or are you really angry because you had a nightmare and you can't express it any other way?

So I take a deep breath and say to my kid, 'It's just water, man.' And my three kids will look at me, wondering, *He's not going to yell at me?*

'Yeah,' I tell them, 'just wipe it up, dude. It's no big deal.'

DUE | Retraining the default mode with meditation
DUE QUACH, SOCIAL ENTREPRENEUR AND REFUGEE

As a person who did due diligence for a living with private equity investments, my job was to sniff out bullshit. If companies were bullshitting us about their prospects or their business plan, then I would try to give them a reality check. I enjoyed that a lot.

Around 2011, I became so intrigued with research showing the health benefits of meditation and about how ancient teachings on mind training lined up with discoveries from neuroscience, that I decided to go to India to gain a direct understanding. I kind of brought the same attitude to it of: if there's some bullshit in this, I'm going to find out. I'm going to know that people are just exaggerating claims, or this is just wishful thinking, or whatever.

I bought a one-way ticket to Dharamsala and spent time at a place called Tushita. That's where I did my first meditation retreat. The founder is a highly regarded master Buddhist teacher named Lama Zopa Rinpoche. When I got there, I heard that he was actually at Tushita on a personal retreat to recover from a stroke.

I was assigned to a dorm room in the meditation hall building on the second floor. My bed happened to be right next to the window. As I was trying to go to sleep, I heard all this chanting. I looked out the window and there was this old fellow who was being supported by attendants and they were chanting something I couldn't understand while they circumambulated the building. I was like, 'Oh my God. That's him. I bet that's him.' I went outside to fill up a water bottle and the Tibetan night guard came over and said, 'Why don't you go join them?' I was like, 'What? Is that allowed?' He said it was, so I just fell in behind them trying to send out positive vibes. I didn't know what they were chanting.

At some point, once we finished all of the ritual, Lama Zopa Rinpoche turned to me and said, 'Who are you?' Then he gave me a teaching that went over my head, and said, 'You're very lucky to find the Dharma (the teachings of the Buddha) and to understand true happiness.' I was thinking, does he not know that I'm an atheist and I'm just here to try to understand what this is about? I don't know what true happiness is and I don't know if I found the Dharma. I'm just curious. I'm just here to learn.

Then a couple of days later, he did a teaching for the class in a question-and-answer style. The first question was, 'What is emptiness?' As he was explaining emptiness, there was suddenly this inner voice within me trying to explain what he was trying to say. I had never really had that experience before, where something inside me was commenting on what someone else was saying. It wasn't in words. It was like pictures. I saw what emptiness was in my mind. Then I suddenly blissed out. I felt like all this energy came into my heart and up through the top of my head, and it felt like I was as big as the room or even bigger.

I was like, *Wow. I don't know what this is, but I'm extremely happy.* I was giddy. I felt so elevated. It was this sense of being beyond time and space and not being limited to my body, even though I had a body, and not understanding how people could be unhappy, because clearly our natural state is being blissed out.

It is hard to describe in language what I experienced. It was such an amazing realisation that at a higher level there was much more to me than could fit in my body. Then I was like, *Is this what he meant to say when he told me that I was lucky to discover the Dharma and true happiness? Did he know that I had no idea what he was talking about then—but now I might?*

For days after, I just couldn't stop smiling. Anything that happened, I just had this glow on my face. I couldn't imagine ever not being happy. It was just the sense that everything would be okay and there was a sense of being beyond everything and yet being there, present in the moment.

Then I went into a Vipassana meditation retreat, a 10 and a half day completely silent retreat, which was a powerful experience after having this taste of what people might call an awakening. The way Vipassana is marketed, it's like the closest thing you can experience to how the Buddha originally taught meditation. After three days of complete silence, focusing on your breath, they then teach you to meditate by scanning your body up and down. What I didn't realise was that when you go through such a long period of sensory withdrawal—you're not reading, not watching TV, you're just turning inwards—you can become super sensitive to all the vibrations in your body.

Later, I had an even more reality-shattering experience in Kolkata. I had been invited there to study a form of energy healing developed by a teacher named Master Choa Kok Sui from the Philippines. A part of the class involves looking at a life-size photo of Master Choa. Then you greet him with respect and say *namaste*, which means, 'I see and honour the divinity within you.'

The first time I did this exercise, nothing happened, I just thought *this is silly. Why the hell did we bother doing this? Just get on with it.* The second time we did it—and I don't know if it was a better, more life-size, more realistic image—I'm not sure what happened, but I remember looking at his image, saying 'namaste', and suddenly his picture became a real being, like in a *Harry Potter* movie.

It came to life and he smiled and winked at me. I was so shocked I nearly fainted. I was just totally stunned and thrown off. I couldn't even pay attention to the rest of the class because things like that aren't supposed to happen. I started wondering, *Maybe I made that up.* I would go back and stare at the picture, thinking if I made it up it could happen again, but it never happened again. Even to this day, I can't explain it with science, except that maybe I wanted to hallucinate so badly that I made it happen. I still don't really understand it.

Months later, I did yoga teacher training and asked the yogi instructing us, who is also a mystic, to explain the difference between my mystical experiences and the Buddha's experience of enlightenment. Was it the same thing? He explained that while the Buddha stayed in that state the rest of his life, most of us touch that state and then come back. We don't stay there, we keep coming back to our everyday consciousness. Sometimes it's easier to do that because you have to navigate the real world, but what made the Buddha special was that he embodied that consciousness and he transmitted that consciousness. I was like, 'Okay, that's a pretty interesting way of looking at what enlightenment is.'

I remember reflecting on that and thinking that there are so many people who have these great highs, these ecstasies from these blissful experiences, and it's almost like doing LSD or marijuana, but then you come back to normal life and you're still an asshole. So, it isn't about levitation or special powers, it's about your ability to stay in that state and not get hijacked by real life, and the normal, everyday sense of being limited and having to be afraid, or having to chase things that give us status in life.

I saw that there were moments in my life where I was still being hijacked by fear and by desire and by greed. The only way to make sense of this was to turn to neuroscience and understand the brain. The Buddha must have done something to his brain that made him more or less immune from the hijacking that I was still going through. I can't say that his life was free from trauma; some accounts of his life say that his mother died giving birth to him. Also, in that period of time in India, there was lots of war and lots of killing, so even though the commonly told story about the Buddha is that his father tried to protect him, it's unlikely that the historical Buddha could've been that sheltered. He seemed to have found a way to heal trauma and to heal his fear and heal his greed.

I started to try to overlay spiritual teachings with what neuroscience said about the brain. My premise was that if something is actually true, science will validate it. It won't be just woo-woo and mystical. It has to hold up logically. It can't just be that this worked for one person yet it can't be replicated. Science is all about replication.

What occurred to me when I was doing the Vipassana meditation was that I wasn't just one person. I saw that I had at least three modes of being. There was the person who was constantly afraid of being left behind, not getting enough food, just afraid for no reason. It was very irrational. Then there was a slightly different energy: the person who chased rewards. I couldn't control it. It was almost a compulsion to want to be at the top of the pyramid. I had no idea why I was doing it.

So I came up with scientific language to match the Buddhist terms. I called the first persona 'Brain 1.0', because it seemed to relate to my freeze, fight or flight type of system. Whenever that got triggered, I would go into that state. Buddhists call it 'the afflictions'. When I'm in Brain 1.0, I'm like a piece of coal, just so dense and hard—I'm blocked. Nothing is flowing. This other persona that's just chasing and jumping through hoops constantly, I called 'Brain 2.0', because it seemed tied to my dopamine system, the reward circuits. Every time Brain 2.0 got set off, I was ready to run any race or do any challenge to win the prize. I was like a bull charging after something. I could be charging after the wrong thing, but I can't course-correct. It's very primal. Buddhists call this *tahna*, or 'craving'.

Then there was this other version of me that could see that whatever that prize was or that hoop was, it wasn't worth it. I didn't really want to chase it. Or that the thing that I was afraid of was irrational and I didn't really have to be afraid. I began to call that 'Brain 3.0', because it seemed to correspond to a more detached way of looking at the world that more closely reflected my core values.

When I'm in Brain 3.0, it's like I'm just space. I'm just awareness. I can see the bigger picture, like the overview effect astronauts talk about. I think most times when we experience wisdom or transcendence, we're experiencing a spiritual overview effect. It's like transmitting a perspective that we mortals don't normally see. The Buddhists would call that *samma ditthi*, which can be translated as 'a higher view'. When I'm in that brain state, I can detach and let go of the thing the charging bull inside me was trying to get. I can make peace with it. When I'm in Brain 3.0, I'm not really controlled by my fear or my cravings or my impulses.

During the meditation retreats I had begun to recognise that I have an inner teacher, like my yoga teachers used to talk about: 'Greet your inner teacher.' I used to wonder, *What is this imaginary friend?* But throughout the Vipassana retreat I felt like this inner teacher was guiding me to have these insights about shifting into these different states and that, being the observer, being detached, having equanimity, are all characteristics of this inner teacher, who I started to call the inner sage.

When I meditated, I saw that I shifted between these three different states, and that I could choose to train my mind to shift into Brain 3.0 to respond to life with compassion and kindness. Then those other parts of my brain would no longer drive and control me.

After a month of retreats, I saw that I didn't want to chase carrots anymore. I could let them go, even if they were dangling in front of me. The once crazy, competitive person was calm. I didn't have to prove myself or show how smart I was. I didn't have to fill up my ego. I was zen—I had never been that way before. I was like, 'Whoa, this is *better* than drugs.'

As a brain geek, my fascination for neuroscience has no bounds. I mean, I could talk about the brain for days, weeks, months, or even years. I realised that meditation did fit with neuroscience: they made sense together. That excited me.

The same way that athletes practise drills, we need to practise how to train our minds when we're in situations that challenge or even torment us, so that we don't sink into the worst possible part of ourselves. We can actually learn how to hold all those responses inside ourselves with compassion, and then transform whatever pain or anxiety we might feel and respond with wisdom—really dig deep and connect to that inner sage.

It's not predetermined that once you experience Brain 3.0 that all the programs in Brain 1.0 or Brain 2.0 are erased. Every time you encounter past conditioning, the programs in 1.0 and 2.0 come back to the surface. Every day, every moment, you have to choose to keep activating Brain 3.0 to create a new habit, to create a new way of responding. That's what helps you break those toxic programs. That's basically what mindfulness is: being able to watch your autopilot and all the ways you've been pre-conditioned with certain habits and patterns, and choose to break those patterns.

In neuroscience, there's this thing called the 'default-mode network'. Your brain is constantly consuming energy, even when you're not focused on any particular task. What it's doing, this default-mode network, is simulating reality, constructing a model of the world inside your head that helps you navigate through this outer world. Sometimes that model is out of date and you can live in a way that's not in sync with larger reality or society. So you have to update your model of the world.

What's interesting about meditation, what scientists have discovered, is that, a lot of the time, these simulations are just stories that we have about how we believe the world works. We don't question them. We just keep running through them mindlessly and we create self-fulfilling prophecies. What mindfulness meditation does is open up your senses so that you're receiving more feedback or more sensory input from the world. You're not imposing your projections of the world on other people. Your default-mode network actually goes quiet and then wisdom kind of just bubbles to the surface in the form of gut feelings.

Even the most famous scientists will say their theories started out as intuitive gut feelings and they followed them, and it opened up this huge breakthrough in science. And if you talk to a scientist, an artist, or any of these people who are acknowledged for being geniuses, many of them say, 'I don't know where it came from. It's like I downloaded it.'

When you meditate, you start to become much more mentally agile. Instead of forcing a story onto a situation, you're just seeing the situation for what it is. And when you're practising sensory awareness, and you're quieting the default-mode network, you're creating an inner calm. Often, when you are meditating, you're activating your parasympathetic nervous system, too. There's a specific nerve, your vagus nerve, that connects your brain to all of your internal organs, including your heart. Every time you tune in to your heart, you elevate vagus nerve activity. That allows you to come out of Brain 1.0 and Brain 2.0. It's sort of all built-in and wired in this very complex biofeedback system. When you're hijacked in a state of stress, the blood flow naturally leaves Brain 3.0, and it's easier to just wallow in Brain 1.0 or go deeper into Brain 2.0 because you're programmed to deepen whatever state you're already in. When you take time to tune in and you activate the vagus nerve, your parasympathetic system, you increase blood flow to Brain 3.0.

If you look at the research and neuroscience of it, and you understand how the default-mode network works, you can retrain your default-mode network with meditation. I'm learning to deactivate it. That's pretty awesome. Most people go to the gym and work out different muscles. I'm like, 'I want to work out different neural circuits. I want to train my brain to be sharper, to be more present. I don't want to be someone whose mind is on something else when you're trying to talk to me.' This is a skill worth cultivating, especially in a world where everyone is on their gadgets all the time.

I feel like meditation is just the practice. It's just the basketball team getting together to shoot hoops, but the real game is the game of life. When you do your training, but then you get out into the real world and all these crazy things happen, are you reverting back to Brain 1.0 or Brain 2.0? Or can you stay centred and be that 'higher self' in those situations and be guided by that inner wisdom that's coming from the universe, through you, into the world? People who can do that, people like Gandhi, Mandela or Martin Luther King, they shine so much light into darkness, and people need them in order to stand up and have the moral courage to say, 'This is enough. We won't accept this anymore. There must be change, because we will not tolerate the status quo.'

Before I learned to meditate, I used to let the darkness take a hold. I wouldn't stand up when I saw things that I didn't agree with. My cynicism gave me a defence. It kept me in survival mode. Things changed when I started to meditate. I became more courageous. It's like I was connecting to a force that was much bigger than me, and it helped me to stand up for what I believe in.

One of my favourite quotes that I came across is from Fr Richard Rohr: 'Pain that is not transformed is transmitted.'[17] I thought, *Wow. That's the story of my life.* I can either transmit pain or transform it. I like myself better when I am able to transform it. Trauma doesn't have to be a life sentence. I am living proof that a person can be a refugee from a war-torn country, grow up in poverty surrounded by violence, suffer PTSD and still beat the odds.

I'm a global citizen. I don't fit any stereotypes. I love science. I love meditation. I love capitalism. I love social entrepreneurship. With enlightened management teams, I believe that business can make the world a better place. I see my life mission to build bridges, bring meditation into the corporate realm, help bosses to embody a higher consciousness, be a portal to help business become a force for good.

With my social enterprise Calm Clarity, I'm attempting to introduce neuroscience along with meditation, to weave the two together to show how the brain works to reach a higher state of functioning and actualisation.

One thing life has taught me is that we must not underestimate the resilience of the human spirit in ourselves and in each other. Overcoming adversity using Brain 3.0 opens a path to enlightenment— that is the key to the portal. For whatever the reason, I am in this body and I'm going through this life on this planet. I need to do my best to make a positive impact on the collective consciousness. When you get the opportunity to make the world a better place, you just can't walk away from it. You have to say, 'Yes, I'm going to do this. Bring it.'

HEATHER | Stillness changed me

HEATHER HENNESSY, FORMER US NATIONAL TRACK
ATHLETE AND SPORTS TV PRESENTER

I never even thought about going back to the cliff where I broke my back. I didn't really know if I ever would. Why would I go back? It was such a painful experience for me. Even the thought triggered stuff in my body in the days leading up to my return. And now I feel this really great sense of peace about it.

When I first stepped on that cliff so many years ago, I wasn't someone who felt empowered at all. I didn't even want to jump, I just did it out of a need to please. So much of my life has been about this need to please other people, to put other people first. I was always worried about other people, men in particular. I picked ones that were abusive, who put me down. I wasn't confident at all. I didn't feel good about myself, but I had these beautiful dreams of running in the Olympics. And I was on the path to doing that. To be able to stand at that cliff again, to look down and think that something beautiful's come out of it, is so powerful.

I'm not someone who ever just naturally or openly expresses emotion. I'm someone who was taught to hold things together. From being an honoured TV personality, to my family, my marriage and all these areas of my life, feeling that I was the one who had to stay strong. No matter what painful things I was going through, I always felt that it was my role. Even though it usually meant ignoring what was really going on for me, on the inside. I had expected that when I stood on the cliff again I would feel a tremendous sadness, mixed with relief, but, when I was actually there, I could not stop crying.

My heart was racing and it was just so much more than I thought it would be.

I said a prayer while I was meditating up there. It's something I've done all my life. *As I stand in front of this cliff, I just ask that please God, Jesus, angels, spirit, everyone from the other side, pour light into me now. Give me pure healing and help release anything that I'm still holding on to from that past experience. Help me release it from my physical body, my mental body, my emotional self. Just help me to fully release it, to let in the light now, to fully heal and to experience a lightness from that, and to be able to move forwards in my path, and in any way that you want my healing to be of help to other people on their healing path. I just let go, and I thank you for this experience. I'm just so grateful. Thank you. Amen.*

I have been thinking throughout the whole process of making the film and working on my book, reflecting on everything, my whole journey. It's been hard not to question things at times and expend a lot of energy asking *why* things happened like they did. At the time, everyone looked at my injury and thought, 'Poor Heather, it's such a tragedy.' But actually, it put me on a path towards what really mattered in life. It was an awful time and it's amazing to see what a blessing it has become. It's made me the person I am. So to be grateful for that experience, instead of feeling frustrated by it, which I did for so long, was incredible and unexpected. One of the greatest moments was stepping up to that spot for the first time since it happened and getting the feeling that everything has been perfect.

Everything I've been through—my hard childhood, breaking my back, a really painful marriage, all these things—I wouldn't really change anything. It's built me into who I am. It's as though if you don't face something, there will always be a question mark: if I hadn't broken my back, would I have moved as far into understanding all of that? I had to hit that deepest low point in order to say, *Okay, I'm either going to completely spiral down, or I'm going to have to figure out a way to get better.* That's what got me into my spiritual life, realising that there's so much more to life than accomplishments and our physical being, and needing to be an athlete to be successful.

You can have all the money in the world, you can have the career, you can keep running out on all your problems, but you're just going to continue running. You're never going to have that sense of self-worth, self-love or just being okay. And you can only depend on your physical body so much because, in a moment, it can be taken away from you. You can be in a car accident, have an injury or an illness. You never know; life is unpredictable.

I really feel for people who are in pain. You feel kind of claustrophobic. You don't want to have to deal with it. That's why I work so hard to be positive and to meditate and find stillness and peace on a level that's not physical. It's vital to my overall wellbeing, because if I just continued to stay in a place of feeling my pain and sulking, then I wouldn't be able to dream and accomplish what I am doing now. I've had tough surgeries, so I know what really bad physical pain feels like, and I have flare-ups sometimes, but emotional pain runs so deep. Emotional scars are worse than physical scars because they stay there a lifetime, unless you really work through them.

Running releases endorphins, but, for me, it was also a form of physical meditation. When you're running, you forget what it is that you're going through. When you're meditating, you're also out of your head. You release your mind and your thoughts, and, in a way, you're floating, too. The difference with running is that you are still so connected to the force of the physical body, whereas with meditation, you're in this relaxed state where you're actually really connected to your inner being.

I was so uncomfortable with stillness at the time of my accident and now I choose it. It was like it was slowly forced upon me until I realised it was stillness that helped me. It helped me to connect with myself.

When I meditate, I have this feeling of leaving my body. It's a feeling of being free, being free from my physicality, no matter what pain I'm going through, no matter what's going on in my life, no matter what my struggles are. It's that feeling of letting go and connecting to the real me, the essence of me. It grounds me, reminds me of why I'm here and how I'm connected to the bigger picture of life. And it's just a beautiful feeling, as if I'm floating in the universe. Often, I see a lot of light. Whenever I'm in that place of stillness I always feel like I see this light, just a big beam of light. And that always instantly puts me in a place of peace.

When I get busy and I don't take time to be still and be with myself, that's when I notice things are chaotic and not going well. That's when things in my life don't line up and I can't hear my intuitive voice as clearly. But my body tries to send me warnings: either I have a physical symptom, or things start to feel overwhelming or stressful. What's worse is that society keeps feeding this idea that we have to be constantly busy and chase success. But that just makes us lose our connection with that voice from within. We are all born with this wonderful guidance system. The voice within is like a map. And stillness is what gives you the ability to read it.

The one thing I've learned through my life is when I go against my intuition, things don't work out. When I follow it, things unfold. Our inner voice never lies. If I could go back in time to that moment at the top of the cliff now, I wouldn't jump. But I had to learn how to speak my truth. It wasn't easy for me. Meditation helped with that. I felt that I had a husband who really didn't want me to use my voice, or to be strong, and, between that and my dad, I had to shut that part of myself down. I had to learn the strength to confront some of that stuff, and the courage to just be myself and not let it hold me back anymore. I still have fearful thoughts and moments, and worries, and all of that. But it's a matter of making the choice to do it anyway, and to accept that there's never going to be a time in your life when those fears, those human things, don't come up. You can still be courageous, though, and do what, in your heart, you know is right.

No matter what has come on my path to make things challenging, I've just never let it stop me. I've consistently tried to have the perseverance, and it hasn't been easy, to keep going and keep dreaming, and keep putting a vision out there that things will continue to come into my life to, you know, create a life that I want for myself. In a year I've turned my life around from feeling depressed following my marriage breakup, and like I was going in the wrong direction, to completely transforming everything.

I finally feel like I'm coming into my own, I definitely do. It's a great feeling to be happy alone, which wasn't the case before. Sometimes I give myself a hug. I just pat myself on the back like, I have your back. I wish I understood the importance of that more in my younger years, because I searched it out so much, wanting it, that support from the people around me. I spent years feeling let down when it didn't come. Now I'm trying to do that for myself. That experience of stillness shifted me, and daily meditation changed my life forever.

I don't consider myself a runner anymore, that's for sure, or an athlete, as I used to define myself. Now I'm just someone who's learning to love myself, which was something I was never taught, or I didn't realise the importance of in the past, but now I know it's a priority. I'm someone who believes more in the things I can't see than the things I see. I'm less worried about my career and more focused on being true to myself and on being a role model—not just for other people but also for myself. I'm not striving for achievements or to run away anymore. Now I'm striving to be fulfilled on a deeper level.

When I was struggling to pick myself up after my accident, all the inspiring stories of transformation that I watched and read made such a difference for me, helping me have humility in my situation and to put things in perspective. Now I'm starting to share my story with others in case it can be that same tool for another person who needs it.

I feel a special calling to work with women to encourage them not to put up with controlling, jealous and abusive behaviour. My vision is to be able to do that in a global way, to help people heal and find a sense of peace and connect to their spiritual life. When I broke my back, I remember saying to myself, *You're going to use this for something good. You just have to believe it.* My mom definitely kept pounding that into my mind, too, saying that all this would be for a bigger purpose.

I'm also working on some illustrated kids books, which is a beautiful thing I never imagined I'd be doing, but I love it. When you're younger and you feel like you have nowhere to turn, I don't know if there's a worse feeling than that. It's what motivates me to help kids with meditation and mindfulness through story. Kids' books are just so great, because you can share messages in a fun and playful way. What's better than teaching kids about mindfulness and how to start down their own spiritual path? I think about what I would have liked to learn at that age, and it flows on from there. I love working with kids. I love working with women. But I want to see everyone live their best life. I want to see a real planetary shift for the better.

JIM | Where our greatest wisdom comes from

JAMES R. DOTY MD, NEUROSURGEON AND NEUROSCIENTIST

When I talk about this woman Ruth, and what she taught me as a child, it was really a form of meditation or mind training. Some aspect of what she taught me is commonly referred to now as mindfulness, but it was more than that. It was this idea of not just sitting with your own internal dialogue and not having an emotional response to it, but also about changing that dialogue, recognising your own suffering and how it limits you and makes you self-focused.

At the time I interacted with Ruth, the terms 'brain neuroplasticity' and 'mindfulness', and even an understanding of how intention and visualisation allow us to create and strengthen neural pathways, were largely unknown concepts. We now know that, through these types of actions, we can create our own reality. The events that happen to us that we create narratives around, they're not real, they're constructs we've created. What people don't realise is they can go back and change that narrative.

I changed my narrative so that I didn't have this emotional attachment to events. It allowed me to look at others and be compassionate. It also allowed me to be present, which gave me the ability to listen and connect. That's truly what gives one happiness, joy and contentment. When you're no longer suffering, when you're no longer focused on your own suffering, there's this sense of lightness.

That profound shift in my perspective as a child ultimately led me to create the Center for Compassion and Altruism Research and Education at Stanford University, where we study the neuroscience of compassion, and the value proposition of being compassionate and how it profoundly affects your mental and physical health in a positive way. How it affects your longevity, and everyone around you—your family, your friends, even strangers—by simply caring. As human beings, our default mode—if you take away the distractions of modern society—is to care for another and, when you authentically care for another, everything works at its best. That's just how we evolved as a species, and it's extraordinary.

I've been blessed with meeting some of the greatest and most profound religious and spiritual leaders, and I'm an atheist. I don't believe in anything except this moment, and people ask me, 'Well, how is it that you've been embraced by these people when you're a complete non-believer?' I say, 'That's not true at all because every one of them, if you really talk to them, it's not about the dogma. It's about whether you have an open heart, whether you're authentic, and whether you are in the present, and it's the present that connects all of these people.'

People ask me about my own meditation practice. It's pretty much the practice we developed at Stanford University, which we validated as affecting you physiologically by improving blood pressure, cardio function and other aspects of health. It's basically four steps:

1) Be present by relaxing your body.
2) Recognise the dialogue and change it.
3) Have self-compassion.
4) Express compassion for all humanity.

Having done this practice for many hours a day for many years, I ultimately integrated it into my daily behaviour and all of my interactions.

Some people who are joyous, who are connected, who are free, haven't done meditation practices because they don't need them. I found that what worked for me and helped me was, initially, doing hours and hours of meditation where I would sit in quietude, and reflect and just sit and experience these visions, these images, these words coming past me and just sit with them. That was extraordinarily helpful, especially when I understood that wasn't even reality, and therefore, my attachment to these things was meaningless.

The other thing I found was that as I did more of that, it became so integrated that every moment became a moment to be mindful, to be thoughtful, and to be self-reflective. My practice now is simply to sit for a brief period in stillness and reflect on the awe and the joy of the world and just simply be present in it. That stillness can even be in a crowd of people; every moment is a moment to be present. It doesn't have to be in the woods necessarily, although that's an extraordinarily wonderful place to connect with nature. Even in a crowded room, you can pause for a moment and just sit and be thankful that you can just be.

As a scientist, sometimes it's hard for me to accept the idea of the existence of an external being, or something that makes these wonderful things happen, and that life isn't just random. But as is the nature of humans, we like to find explanations about things that happen to us. So, when something good happens to us, we say, *It was because I was good and I deserved it.* And if something bad happens, often we internalise it and think, *I deserved it.*

All of us love it when we get accolades, when we receive awards, when people tell us what we've accomplished. It feels really good. Something else that I've learned from spiritual leaders is that having attachment to that experience is just as bad as having attachment to negative experiences, and this is where this idea of equanimity comes into play, this idea of having an evenness of attitude about the world where you're not constantly thinking, 'I want this to happen to me so I feel good,' or, 'Jeez, this bad experience has happened to me and I want to run away as quickly as possible.' Simply to have a calmness about you, whether you're up or down, and not be having an emotional reaction, but understanding that all of these things are transitory. Developing this equanimity is one of the biggest challenges we have and one of the greatest gifts.

And I think the reason spiritual and religious leaders, whether it's the Dalai Lama, Desmond Tutu or Shri Shri Ravi Shankar, et cetera all have this type of persona about them—they exude calm and radiance and acceptance, while they navigate these incredible peaks and troughs—is that none of them have become stuck in the places we regularly get stuck in. They have been able to stay in a place of peace.

In the presence of individuals like that, you immediately know that you are loved, you are embraced completely, without their need to think whether you deserve it or not. And when you receive that from them, when you're in their presence and you feel that, do you know what suddenly happens? There is suddenly a lightness, and there is a joy.

So many of us project the version of ourselves that we want people to believe. And we remove all the parts in that projection that we don't want others to see. But that's not us, and that projection doesn't allow someone to see us completely, clearly, as who we really are, with all of our flaws, our failings and our shadow.

Many of us have created prisons for ourselves, brick by brick, based on interpretations, judgements, believing when people have told us we're not good, we're not worthy. We believe so firmly that the walls that surround us are real, that we don't even see that we're in a prison. It limits our vision because we can only see what's inside the walls, whether it's our own suffering, the baggage we're carrying, or the pain. So when we do these practices, when we sit in deep contemplation, focus the mind and meditate, and we're able to open the prison door, lightness, joy and abundance are there.

The nature of our humanity is that we will experience pain, but it's how you react to the pain, and that pause before our reaction to that pain, that is the place where we determine our response. That's the place where our freedom lies. There are so many challenges for people with their upbringings, with interactions with their parents, or a sibling, or a friend, and that has caused them great suffering, like it did for me, that they still haven't dealt with. My experience is that people's suffering actually has made them who they are today, and many, if not most, people want to be the person they are today. For most of us, though, it's a process, and while there may be periods where you feel down in life, almost invariably you come back up to a baseline.

I can still be distracted. I'm a human being, and you know human beings are frail, and they're fragile, and we make mistakes. When you think you're beyond that, that's when you'll fall.

The key is really to understand that every interaction, everything that happens is a wonderful, joyous part of life. And the greatest gift you have, that you can give to another person, is to share that joy with them.

AMANDINE | Inner peace brings world peace

AMANDINE ROCHE, HUMAN RIGHTS EXPERT

In a long letter to Ban Ki-Moon, Secretary-General of the UN, who was my director in New York, I asked, 'Are you aware of the mental health conditions of the aid workers in a war zone? If you are aware, what are you doing about it? If you are not aware, can we have a discussion?'

To my surprise, he replied and asked me to come to his office.

I explained about my work in Afghanistan, and about the sanity of my humanitarian colleagues working on the front line. He said, 'We are aware, but we don't know what to do'. Apparently they received resignation letters on a daily basis.

I explained to his team that I had spent 10 years healing myself from all the trauma I'd been through in war zones, including in Afghanistan. They needed to be aware that this was a big issue. I said, 'My colleagues are either depressed and anxious, taking antidepressants, or wanting to commit suicide.'

The team asked, 'What do you propose?'

'Every time I go to the Google offices,' I replied, 'everybody is super happy and healthy. At the UN, we're not like that. We're working for peace in the world, but we don't incarnate what we're preaching. Why don't we try to introduce tools of inner peace, a sort of 'search inside yourself' program?'

They said, 'Okay, go for it.'

So I spent a year studying neuroscience, emotional intelligence, conscious leadership, mindfulness—the cleverest stuff—on a scholarship from the Search Inside Yourself Leadership Institute created by a Google engineer. We needed a program for stress management that was adapted to the humanitarian working on the front line, so we designed a program called the Inner Peacekeeping Program, where we teach the tools of inner peace and resilience to humanitarians in order for them to avoid burnout, PTSD and depression, and to really incarnate peace.

I raised the money to hire a mindfulness teacher, a mental health specialist, a graphic designer and a curriculum teacher, and we designed the whole curriculum. Now we're teaching the program across the Middle East, in Lebanon, Jordan and Libya, to all the humanitarians on the front line who are working with Syrian refugees, and it's been a big success.

In Afghanistan, every day at 6 am I taught yoga and meditation in my garden. Everybody in the area was showing up and I never knew who they would be: Afghan or international. For one hour, we did yoga followed by 30 minutes of meditation. It was the best way to start the day. I watched people's lives transform.

When I started the yoga and meditation in Afghanistan, I had such amazing feedback. As I was doing yoga with women in shelters, I realised that they were completely disconnected—mind from body—and, just by doing some flexibility exercises, I could see on their faces that they felt alive again. They realised that their bodies didn't have to suffer in pain.

One woman was celebrating her husband's birthday in a restaurant outside Kabul. Three people wearing burkas came inside, but it was the Taliban in disguise, and they started shooting everybody in the crowd. They assassinated her husband right in front of her. She got a bullet in the eyebrow and she was bleeding. She took the blood and smeared it on the faces of her three daughters. For the next 10 hours or so, while the Taliban was still shooting around, they lay perfectly still and pretended they were dead. She witnessed many Afghans at the party jump into the lake, but they didn't know how to swim, so they drowned. They just floated on the lake.

When she came to my house, she hadn't slept for 42 days. I asked her to close her eyes and I started to teach her mindfulness meditation. She said, 'Sorry, I cannot close my eyes, because every time I close my eyes I'm back at the restaurant.'

I said, 'That's fine. We're going to do it with our eyes open. What do you hear?'

She said, 'I can hear the birds singing.'

'What do you see in front of you?'

She said, 'I can see the flower blossoming.'

'What do you feel on your bare foot?'

'I can feel the wet grass.'

As I watched, her face, though it was very tense, started to open up. She called me the following day to say it was the first time she had managed to sleep. This is the power of mindfulness. That very simple technique of learning how to just be in the here and now. That's what peace is about.

Honestly, it doesn't cost anything. Americans spent one trillion dollars in Afghanistan in the war. War doesn't bring peace, obviously. It doesn't cost anything to teach a person how to breathe, how to be present, but it brings them peace of mind. When you are at peace with yourself, you raise the level of consciousness of your family and your society. It's very simple, actually.

I wanted to go to Pul-e-Charkhi jail, which is the jail outside Kabul that holds all the criminals and anyone from Al Qaeda or the Taliban. It's the toughest jail in Afghanistan. My aim was to go there to teach meditation. I went to see the Minister of Defence, and I asked him if he could give me access to the jail. He said, 'Sure. What do you want to do there?'

'Teach meditation to the prisoners,' I said.

He said, 'What is meditation?'

I said, 'Okay, is there a cushion in your office? Why don't you sit on the cushion and I'll teach you?' I did a 20 minute meditation with him.

When I looked at his face afterwards, I saw how relaxed he was.

He said, 'I have never felt so good. I will give you the key to Pul-e-Charkhi on one condition. Could you teach meditation to my wife, because I cannot bear her anger?'

I said, 'Sure.' So, I went to his house and taught meditation to his wife.

It was amazing to watch the minister so open to meditation and to see an immediate transformation. He said, 'I should do it more, because I'm kind of a target for the Taliban, so if I come to my office and I do this meditation every day, I will be more relaxed and less stressed.'

One time I talked to a Taliban commander who really touched my heart. I checked his profile on Wikipedia before meeting him and realised that he was a real criminal. He had been with the mujahedeen before, and was very close to Bin Laden. He came into my office because now he wanted to be a democrat.

He was scared that because of all the corruption, he would never win the election to become the Deputy of Zabul. I asked him, 'Why do you want to be a democrat with such a background?'

To my surprise, he said, 'Because of my daughter. At school, my daughter got bullied by the other kids because her father is a criminal, and I don't want my daughter to have this impression of me. I want her to know that I'm a good father who works for peace and democracy now.'

I asked him, 'Do you meditate?'

He said, 'No. What is it?'

I said, 'It's like the prayer, like you pray five times a day. You reconnect.'

And he said, 'Teach me.'

He invited me to his house and I remember, even when I came, he said, 'Be careful that people don't see you coming to my place,' because he's a former Taliban. He said, 'Usually I don't receive foreigners.'

I went with a translator because he spoke Pashtu, and I taught him meditation. He loved it so much. I could see on his face that he was so peaceful. He asked me to teach meditation to his kids.

He called all his kids around him—maybe six, seven, a lot of kids—and he said, 'Now you listen to what the woman has to tell you, because it's very important.' We were in a circle and we all meditated together in the living room. It was such a beautiful moment, because I realised that there is no border, there is no frontier with meditation. When you really reach this peace of mind, it's pure bliss.

When I went to teach at the juvenile jail in Kabul, Bagram, I spoke with the kids who were under 18 and I asked, 'Why are you here?' Some of them had been trained in the madrasa school to become suicide bombers, others had done burglary and different types of crimes. I taught them meditation and, at the end, they said, 'Thank you, madam, because I realised just now that what I was doing was not okay. We were so brainwashed that we were sure we were right and it was right to kill. But now that I have reconnected with my heart, I realise that no, no it was not okay.'

For the program now, I'm teaching refugees, which gives me so much joy because I teach them techniques to heal from PTSD and burnout. The Jordanian and Lebanese women have also really touched my heart. So many of them contacted me afterwards saying, 'You changed my life because now I do my breathing techniques every day, when I go to work, when I deal with my family, when I have a strong emotion, I pause, I meditate, I reflect and I answer mindfully, consciously.'

Step by step, you realise, *Yeah, I want to work for peace, but by teaching this curriculum and these techniques, I am making a more significant contribution to peace.* I do hope that one day big organisations like the European Commission, the UN and all the NGOs hire people based not only on their IQ, but based on their emotional intelligence, on their social intelligence, on what makes them human and what work they have done on themselves to incarnate peace, to be authentic, and to be a soldier of peace. A soldier of nonviolence. To be a role model.

You have to be a role model, and in order to be a role model, you must work on yourself. You have to be aware of who you are, what your life purpose is, what your mission is, and how you are going to contribute to the world with your gifts. That's it. You can only do that when you have peace of mind.

These practices changed my way of serving when I'm on a mission. I went from my head to my heart and I realised that I needed to live in true tolerance and compassion to be a real advocate of peace. To me, this is the way you should hire a humanitarian, and my wish is that each organisation will have a department of wellness and mindfulness, where we can assign actual budget to this kind of program. Right now, there is not a single penny for that, but these organisations are starting to become aware that it should be a higher priority.

The idea for starting my own foundation came to me during my meditation. At the time, I couldn't understand why the words 'inner peacekeeping' were coming up again and again during my meditation, but now I get it. Now I know why. Initially, I created the Amanuddin Foundation in Afghanistan, and now my new program, the Inner Peacekeeping Program, operates worldwide.

Meditation puts you back on track and helps you to tame your mind—your monkey mind, as the Buddhists say. After I started to practise meditation, it was like I was no longer stuck in the past or in the future. I was able to fully reconnect with the present moment. Right now, there is no trauma, and right now, there is no drama, and right now, there is no pain and suffering. It all belongs to the past. This helps you to turn the page and live your life.

It's interesting, now it's my French government that has come back and asked if I could implement the program for soldiers, so there was definitely a shift of consciousness. There are so many scientific studies now that prove meditation helps you to recover from trauma and from PTSD. It's a wave, and the wave started in India, moved through California, and now it's reaching Europe and the Middle East as well.

It was the former UN Secretary General Dag Hammarskjöld who renovated the meditation room at the UN headquarters. In one of his speeches, he emphasised that each UN staff member should take time to sit in silence and stillness, and reconnect with themselves to better serve the world.[18] He got it, and, with the curriculum, I just woke up his legacy.

I'm creating this training program to avoid future humanitarians becoming as traumatised as I was. I don't want them to suffer as much as I suffered. So the Inner Peacekeeping Program is to give the humanitarians the tools of inner peace, and to help them cope with all the stress they face on a daily basis. It provides a model of mindfulness, emotional intelligence, conscious leadership, neuroscience, meditation and yoga. In the program, we look at what it means to work for the UN, what it means to work for peace, and how you can connect the mind with the body. It's a very complete program in three days, followed by one month online where we train people to create a habit and put into practise the 20 inner peace tools we've taught them.

Everyone who completes the program must be selected by their supervisor, otherwise it's voluntary. Sometimes there's a long waiting list. The supervisor prioritises those who work in refugee camps.

We're in Libya, Lebanon and Jordan. We're going to Syria and to Iraq. I'm also planning to go to African countries, like Kenya, Sudan, Somalia, South Africa, Congo and Mali, where there are many crises with refugees. The Amanuddin Foundation is for Afghanistan and the Inner Peacekeeping Program is for all the other countries.

For me, that's real peace. There's no other way. I've been working on the peace process, democratisation and human rights for almost 20 years, and I have learned that peace is not in the head. Peace is in the heart. Einstein said, 'The longest way in the world is from the head to the heart.' This is the longest way to peace, too. You can train the brain and learn about democratisation and human rights, but if you don't incarnate those within yourself, you are a fraud.

I changed my life with 10 days of Vipassana meditation. I spent the first three or four days in the past, reliving it, and, after three days, in the future. The final day, I broke the wall of silence and went outside. After spending 11 hours a day meditating—living in a world of silence where you don't write, you don't read, you don't have eye contact—I was in such a deep, deep state of meditation that I felt like a diver. I went deep within myself to reach a place where I was so at peace. It was an amazing transformation for me. Now when I meditate, I know where I can go within myself to find that spot, that place that gave me joy and nurtured my soul. It's like a well. You dig, dig, dig for water then you finally find it. This was when I had the vision to create the Inner Peacekeeping Program.

If you ask me whether I miss Afghanistan, the answer is, 'Of course.' It's a big part of my heart because it led me to my inner peace, which I had spent years looking for.

Now my priority is to make sure I have enough budget to develop the Inner Peacekeeping Program to hire more trainers to teach and bring more mindfulness with my French government, with the military, and at UN headquarters. It is my big dream to make sure that the UN signs a resolution to develop a budget for mindfulness and wellness.

My number-one priority for world peace is to focus on inner peace. My wish is that everybody finds this stillness within themselves because, honestly, when you reach this peace point, you're not going to kill your neighbour, you're not going to fight with your husband; you're at peace, and so you contribute more peace to the world because you're at peace with yourself. That's how it works.

Even if the world is at its craziest point to date, I can see so much awakening all around. More and more people are meditating. More people are practising conscious eating, more conscious everything. People are joining the wave, and it's so beautiful to observe.

RONNIE AND KITRA | It was a special time, where I entered into still time

RABBI RONNIE CAHANA AND KITRA CAHANA, PHOTOGRAPHER AND DOCUMENTARIAN

Authors' note: Here, we meet Rabbi Ronnie Cahana with Kitra Cahana, one of his daughters. Their story commences in crisis, as Kitra recounts her first visit to the hospital following her father's stroke and how, in that moment, everything changed.

Kitra shared the initial months of recovery with Ronnie in the hospital, and has given form to her father's inner and outer journey to rebuild himself physically via a 'stillness-in-motion' photographic art style that she created in response to his condition. His slowed speech and inner stillness inspired the breathtaking work.

They converse with each other through words and through time; the relationship between them is a dance of life. The following excerpt includes exchanges between the two and is an intimate look into the healing process, not just for Ronnie, but for his family and community as a whole. Theirs is a story of transformation through crisis, and of creation out of catastrophe. Ronnie's words are indented.

When we first came in … I was distraught. I had been out on an assignment working in America and had to fly home to Montreal. The entire airplane ride, I just cried and cried and felt like disaster had struck.

I had a nightmare the night I heard about the stroke. My father came to me in my dream—he was completely fine physically, but his entire persona had changed. He'd turned into a really ugly person, a person who laughed when I was crying and mocked me, and he said: 'I've lived all these years of elegance and now my real persona is going to come out.' That was my dream the first night, and I woke up crying. So I came into the room in that state, with that thought in my mind that I'd lost everything, I'd lost my closest friend. And that just wasn't at all what had happened. It was the complete opposite. So when he responded with love and compassion and blessing, I just felt relief, like I haven't lost anything. And that's also how he felt—that he hadn't lost anything.

> I woke up in stillness and it was wonderful for me. It was really a great gift from the distortions and the hushings of the exterior world.

It wasn't like I went home that night or the next day or the next day … I walked into that room and it was a new existence. At least in those initial months, we lived it together.

> No one loves so full-heartedly as you do, Kitra. It's an immeasurable power that you have.

I felt like, and I've always felt like, I gave everything in those few months.

So beautiful. Greatest gift is your heart ... full heart.

So our time in the hospital became one of just being together and abundance, navigating the hospital system together. Learning about strokes and learning about how to communicate. There were lots of very different lessons that we learned.

My father talked a lot about attunement—we had to attune. In moments when I tried to navigate the hospital system, he would direct me back, saying, 'No, you're not being attuned. We have to attune, we have to become one, you have to be my voice. You have to become my body.' So it was very personal, very intimate, just letting go of yourself in the service of another. It was a special time, where maybe I entered into the slow time that he talks about: *still time*.

> During the stroke, while I struggled to wake up, the lure
> of the siren song from Kitra was the recurring sentence
> from our morning prayers. Kitra's song is the most heavenly
> song I've ever heard. So gentle. ♪♫ *My God, the soul that you*
> *gave me is pure.* ♪♫ Over and over again, in Hebrew. Kitra
> sang it to me so that I absorbed it—first into the heart and
> then it entered my consciousness. I rolled out of my stupor
> through her voice. It's a longer prayer, but she sang just that
> line. Eastern tradition says the wisdom is from the heart.

His initial response was one of creation. Immediately, all he wanted to do for hours and hours each day was just compose. Compose poetry, compose sermons, letters, eulogies. It was like this endless need to express and create, to put into words what he was experiencing, to let all of that out. All of the nursing staff there would insist, again and again, 'Just speak in shorthand, blink once for yes, blink twice for no.' That's what they wanted from us, to be efficient with our time, and my father, he just wanted to be flowery. He wanted to, you know, make jokes. Long jokes. And we were communicating blink by blink.

> Inside me, I feel my full power. I can't translate it, but it's all familiar to me. It's exciting. I lose what I gain if I get lazy, but the power inside is purely present, so I know it will come back. I just need diligence. There are so many things to think of ... the most important for me is voice. To communicate is bringing my heart, my insides, out. Being able to connect and to be understood has to come first, for a Rabbi especially. But this is a new effort, a completely physical effort. To breathe and to phrase correctly, it's exhausting.
>
> I was an athlete in my youth—the body remembers. I had strength and I still have this intensity internally, but it doesn't translate now to the outside. I can't move with the fluidity that I always knew. But the strength is no different. I imagine myself as a seed does, patient beneath the earth, envisioning itself as a tree. And the sensation that began when I was underground was that my head exploded and my limbs just separated from my core body and all my work that I still had to do was to bring my limbs back. I thought that I was lying in my backyard

and calling to my right arm, which was a mile away down the road, and my left arm—another mile in the opposite direction. It was all very clear. The leg was on the other side of town and the other leg—I called them to come together, back to my centre. My calling slowly happened: they came.

There are other even more peculiar sensations. The mind can recreate any stories, just like our dreams. The mind has this tremendous, tremendous awareness of other dimensions. So that's how I got the capacity to turn my neck muscles back too. All of this was impossible, to open my mouth was miraculous. I guess I was a ventriloquist but these were impossible advances—initially I only had the blinks in both eyes.

People often come up to me and say: 'Oh your father, he's such an inspiration.' I always think ... it's just him. I feel like the stroke helped him sharpen his focus. It allowed him to inhabit his beliefs, embody his beliefs, in a way that was really evident to the world around him.

The intensity of the stroke accelerated my understanding of how our sources prop us up to handle anything. To explore the world from this angle, it's very much a beautiful privilege. In life, everything, ultimately, is a privilege—to experience your own personal story and the adventure it takes you on. I get to see things so starkly in contrast to what the normal world lives. I see each profound, new, microscopic insight. I just go at a different pace.

I think my father has always lived on extremes, and he loves living out his own mythology … he loves his own life story. It's an extreme situation and I wouldn't expect him to have reacted in any other way. My mother says he has a healthy ego and he adamantly lives his own existence and never allows anyone else to define it or to create the narrative. So I don't know if it's inspirational, or more of, like, an extreme stubbornness to be oneself. And I think the stroke gave him more space and permission to be fervently himself.

> In my synagogue they told me, 'You're still my Rabbi, nothing's changed.' That's such an honour to hear 'cause I didn't think I had any presence left. It's such a beautiful community. My children told me I'm their father. All that gave me so much life. They restored me. I never lost anything. My wife told me we never separated, so my reality is not what I'm not. They told me who I am still.
>
> Everything is a miracle if you want it to be. Anything. Only, it's up to you if you're surprisable or not. It's your choice, but I've made myself easily surprisable and now it's all wonder and first steps. It's great for me. When you get jaded, you lose curiosity, and then you age. But if you're curious, there are always beginnings. It's the pleasure of being.

It was very clear to me right from the beginning that what was going on here was special. I was floored by my father's response to his condition and the number of people who were coming and looking for comfort from him, the way he would create these reciprocal relationships of giving and healing, and how he demanded that kind of reciprocity in his space. So I knew there was something to create out of this space and to create it together. I had my camera there, and I wanted to document what was happening.

> I don't know if I help people at all—I don't know
> that—but I do know that I'm so thankful that people
> allow me to try to help. It is, to me, the definition of
> love. We need each other to spur [us on] towards more.
> That's why we take the next breath, for more. We humans
> are so easily corruptible and we're so frail, so delicate
> and susceptible to things that are our opposites. We
> have that component in us not to grow. I look to find
> the impetus to continue. Going beyond ourselves,
> our own small limitation shouldn't stop our growth.
> Everything I think about humanity is relational,
> and so that's what we're taught, that for spousal love,
> for family, closeness, it's always dedicating yourself to
> the other that gives meaning in life—I understand it now.
> In the old days, I didn't have to think about it, I could
> *do* it, but now, since I don't have a body, I have closeness
> to the longing for each other, the longing for love. It's a
> beautiful, beautiful inner world that circles inside. I love
> the privilege of this closeness to the people I have such
> a cherished dearness to. That's the physicality of love,
> even over distance. It's our most powerful truth about
> our own self-love.
> It's much more important to know how deeply
> you can love, you're able to love—by inspiration of the
> other—than to be loved. Of course, it's so mutual, but

I'm so thankful that I know eternality through love. The infinite, the godliness, the Paradise to heaven, the Garden of Eden is always pre-glimpsed when we love wildly or beyond ourselves. We only get glimpses of the Garden of Eden (says our Torah) but, because of that, we know that we can always return there. And that's overcoming the exile. So my little exile is irrelevant. The infinite love that's inside our person, our humanity, and our world. The whole world has that.

People talk about art as being therapeutic. It's not exactly that it's therapeutic, but it's just that part of the way I like to exist is in a mode of collaboration and creation. So I started photographing as I would any other story, any other situation I happened to find myself in. And the images were so flat. The images that I took captured the love, they captured what was happening in our room, but I would show them to people and they would go, 'Awww, so sad.' They wouldn't know how to respond. It *seemed* sad. The images felt two-dimensional to me. They were beautiful in and of themselves, but they only went so far and I didn't feel like they matched the power of my father's words. So I really felt like I had to find a visual vocabulary that evoked what we were experiencing, the depth of what we were experiencing, and the height of what we were experiencing. I needed to have images that immediately took the viewer to a place of stillness in the way that his words also brought people to that very same place.

So I started searching and experimenting and playing with my photography, and also really respecting this idea, which my father communicated, of 'slow time'. Really waiting for the right images, really waiting, slowly, to add one more image to the story.

Out of all the projects I've ever done, I think this is the slowest and the longest. We'll carry on this collaboration until one of us dies, and we'll keep writing and documenting this slow time—I call the project *Still Man*. It's a way for us to continue what we started in the ICU [Intensive Care Unit] and the hospital room when we were attuning. So we're attuning our artistic selves together in this collaboration, and this is what I see as our forever project.

Do you feel that?

> Thank God.

Do you like how the images capture you?

> You created my world ... to grow into. It showed me what I looked like.

Do the images describe your inner world? The layering? The slowness?

> It's the world I want. It's perfect. You made that tangible, Kitra. I'm so grateful.

That's what I'm trying to capture.

> You know my soul. It's instinct. Father, daughter.

It's intergenerational. Most of this artwork visually comes from my grandmother's work. She's a Holocaust survivor and she painted her experiences, and I grew up surrounded by that artwork and that voice. So I think, when I'm searching and yearning for my personal artistic voice, that's where I'm looking. I'm looking to her for guidance. My father's poetic voice is also a kind of pastiche of words and layers that wash over a person. I think it's a good match. What I love so much about using his voice in my artwork, his physical voice, is the slowness of it. It really draws me in. It kind of balances with the images, and also the videos. The videos are also very slow-moving. And that's the goal: to open up a space for another time, a passageway to slow down.

Both our parents have been very encouraging that we all return to our lives, to come back and check in and help where we can, but I think it would have been selfish of him to ask me to stay in his slow time forever. But we will always have that touchstone, that shared experience of knowing what it's like to be on that brink of life, and not life, and to come back together.

> In my mind, stillness lets us reflect, but then, after stillness there is something greater: I believe that's our reverence. When we express reverence, to the greatest awareness of less of me and more of the things that are, that we revere, we've reached past ourselves into another. And that's what I look for when I meet people: 'What do you revere? Teach me and share. I'm with you.' And you literally offer everything up.
>
> Mutual vulnerability is all that I ask, from soul to soul, mutual vulnerability. It's the most honest way to live, the courageous way to live. Fear of fear is our problem. With our vulnerabilities, we help each other—love is giving your fears over to someone else.

In Judaism, to be god-fearing is to be humble enough to say to god, 'Help,' as people don't know that strength. It's too much of the lone ranger mentality. We need each other and that's a beautiful truth to say: 'I need help. Please, dear God, one more chance.' That was my prayer when I was unconscious. I had a recurring mantra. I prayed to God, 'Just one more kiss to Karen, please. Please, one more embrace to my children.' And 'Each child needs just one more evidence of eternal love. One more.' And God gave me a full lifetime to continue. I am so, so grateful. I have so many kisses that I got again. So thankful.

The greatest thing we can say to each other is, 'I need you.' That's why adolescents always beat up on their parents by saying, 'I don't need you.' Because they need them so very much. My mother loved me so much because in Auschwitz the world said to her, 'You don't exist at all.' And everything about me and my brothers and my sister's birth was, 'I exist now, to you.' That's how we were treated. I know unconditional love. She was only a 15-year-old child when death was everywhere, in every direction, and she and her sister survived simply because that love was unbreakable, unchallenged, undamageable. A great, great thing it is to love.

I know when I dream deeply and there's a message, so I tell my dream to Karen and she finishes the dream. We've been doing it all our married life. It's a real awareness of the magic of our love. Don't take it for granted.

Before the stroke, I was restless. I was very restless before. And I was in danger, that the angers I saw around me didn't penetrate into me. I didn't have defences before—no armour or shields to separate from the toxicity of anger. Anger is pure selfishness: pretending that we don't deserve to be frustrated or disappointed—no one is immune. And it was horrible to be exposed in societies where anger is the capital of people's interactions. Praise God, I learned to have fortitude against that poison. It pollutes us. That's what the stroke allowed. Even after the stroke I fought the lesson—I made a terrible mistake—but I came, over time of really embracing stillness, to see the misjudgement of character that anger puts into us that blinds us to our cleansing. The stroke was a necessary purge. I am so thankful for this lesson. I am so thankful that I didn't die so that I could learn this.

We were created for joy. We were created to give joy. Love is joy. Love is endless joy. Everything profound—the beauty of life, the awareness of God in your life, the wonder of being, the innocence of perfection—it's only joy. It's the tool to bring closeness. It bridges distance and it gives us the truth that we are needed in the world. Happiness is believing in your life force. It is your life force. We shouldn't squander it.

Many people with locked-in syndrome have only one eye free from paralysis. I've met them. But I've also met a person who rides a bicycle and is completely returned. He came to visit me in the hospital. I said to him, 'Do one

thing for me. Dance with your wife.' He said, 'I don't dance.'
I just looked at him and said, 'Dance with your wife.' They
began to waltz and they were really so happy and I cried
with joy. Life is made for dancing. When people trust that
their bodies can heal themselves, that their bodies can
teach and they can enter stillness, stillness is a wondrous
state. And it touches a truth. To dance again with Karen
is my deepest, deepest anticipation. And I know we will.
And so I think a great work is to teach yourself to get rid
of doubt. Doubts are cripplers; shoo them away, send them
out. Don't have doubts. That's where we are what we
believe and we can choose belief, and that's freedom.

I always ask people, 'What's your paralysis?'. I always
ask. We all have malady and people tell me. It's liberating.
My paralysis is pretty expressed. I don't feel I'm locked in.
I feel I've lucked out. It gives me so much. I see a projection
of myself and I'm just watching. I'm on the front row,
watching this personal revival. It's a brilliant time.

'Oneness is the goal.'

RABBI RONNIE CAHANA

CONCLUSION

There is an experience of interconnectedness (with other people, with the planet) that starts to build over time as a result of practices like mindfulness and meditation, when we spend time in stillness, and from a deep connection to our heart. It's similar to what astronauts refer to as the 'overview effect', which is a shift—or expansion—of perspective that occurs instantaneously when they look back at planet earth for the first time. Suddenly, instead of seeing borders and boundaries, or politics and cultures, or the minutiae and daily chaos of our lives, all they see is a perfectly beautiful, vibrant ball of life, suspended in the vastness of space. What results is a spontaneous cognitive shift. Instead of seeing themselves as individuals, they feel—emotionally, viscerally—part of a whole, part of a single, synchronous community co-existing with nature and the rest of the universe. It's an experience of unity—of 'oneness'—that stirs the depths of their very being, and is exactly the kind of shift we all need to experience to ensure a brighter future, not to mention our survival.

For a long while, we were in touch with several astronauts about possibly appearing in the film and book. Alas, sometimes even beautiful ideas can slip away, but in the process of those conversations and research, we heard American NASA astronaut Dr Mae Jemison refer to a Hindu legend she'd been told as a child, which we feel superbly sums up our world in its current state.

The story takes place in a long-forgotten time, when humans had become so abusive of their divinity that Brahma, the chief god, decided to take their divinity away and hide it. Brahma didn't want them ever to find it again—knowing humans, they would just fall back into the same abusive pattern—so he called a council of the gods to help him decide where to put it. Some suggested he bury it deep in the earth, but Brahma rejected this idea because humans would just dig into the earth and find it. The council suggested sinking it in the deepest ocean, but Brahma knew that humans would learn to dive into the ocean. The gods proposed hiding it at the top of the highest mountain, but Brahma again said no; eventually, humans would climb every mountain. It seemed like humans were capable of eventually reaching everywhere on earth. So, the gods gave up. But Brahma continued to think deeply and finally came upon the answer: he would hide the humans' divinity deep within their own being, because it was, surely, the one place humans would never think to look. And ever since, the story goes, humans have been tirelessly digging, diving, climbing and exploring—searching for something that is actually already inside them.

As a civilisation, we have trodden a lot of paths to find that 'thing' that will give us the wealth, happiness, love and sense of connection we crave, and that we know deep down is our birthright. This exploration has led our species to incredible knowledge and capabilities—a huge asset as we face our current global situation, even though we may not always have found what we were truly looking for. But a change is sweeping through. Increasingly, as we exhaust our external search, we are learning to look inwards to explore the next frontier: our inner space.

By virtue of us being here on earth—now—we are all part of something imminent. A phase shift up to the next level for our civilisation will come through each and every one of us making our own small changes and adding a window of stillness to our day. One of Tom's teachers once said, 'Peace on earth, one meditator at a time.' We can't take responsibility for the choices and actions of others, but we can take responsibility for our own. Meditation can play a key role in helping us do that, giving us the capacity to meet our personal and global challenges head on: we can become exponentially adaptable to meet the needs of the time. It doesn't take much. Just as the Bedouin guide said to Jacqui: 'Close your eyes and open your mind.' The decision to do this is only a matter of time. So as we tremble on the brink of this evolutionary phase shift, contemplating some of our most daunting present-day challenges, we invite you to feel the potential for our species if we take time for stillness, and for our own ability to change the world from the inside out. This is our evolution.

To share in this game-changing—yet incredibly simple—global community experience, join us at www.entertheportal.com, where you will find out more about meditation, transformation and upcoming events.

'Time is just another embrace …

of realising life is coursing through us.'

RABBI RONNIE CAHANA

AN INTRODUCTION TO MEDITATION

BY TOM CRONIN

'Meditation has been around for thousands of years. It's an incredible and profound tool, and what it does is it directs and refines human attention.' MIKEY SIEGEL

Meditation is no different from our phones, our social media or even our problems. All of these are pulling our mind's attention in a particular direction. However, where meditation differs is that it redirects our attention from the outer world to the inner world. From the moment we're born, our mind projects externally to the world around us, processing information each and every day. As we consume this information, it starts to form our identity, as we saw in the stories throughout the book. From an early age, each of our experiences starts imprinting on us and, before long, our malleable brain has been coded by these experiences, which stick with us as we set off on our life course.

When we begin meditating, we reverse the direction of the mind's attention and move it inwards. This is not the natural direction for the mind to move. The mind is constantly seeking stimulation, and thinking about the world around us creates excitement for the mind that's remarkably charming. The outer world is full of all sorts of glamorous and exciting propositions for the mind, so why wouldn't it want to move in that direction? Each thought triggers a sensation shift in the body, and this feeling in the body is a fluctuating pleasure–pain dynamic. Some thoughts trigger pleasurable sensations and some thoughts trigger painful sensations. The mind isn't concerned whether it's pleasurable or painful, it's only seeking excitation of some sort. We move up and down through these peaks and troughs throughout our waking day.

When the mind goes inwards, to the inner silence, beyond thought, a de-excitation occurs. Deepak Chopra, a bestselling author, doctor, speaker and meditation expert says, 'Meditation is not a way of making your mind quiet. It's a way of entering into the quiet that's already there—buried under the 50,000 thoughts the average person thinks every day.'[19] As the mind moves away from the thoughts and into that quiet, we experience a restfulness in the body. This reduced stimulus of the mind translates to reduced stimulation of the body and a physiological and mental state of rest is achieved. One of the great challenges with embracing a daily meditation practice is how much we are drawn to the state of excitation by the outer world. Catching up with friends, going to the movies, making money, reading emails and scrolling through social media feeds are all highly stimulating things that few people have the inclination to turn their backs on in order to explore their inner world.

What *is* compelling people to look inwards today is a need, a deep need, to take time out and recover from the overloading effect that this ever-increasing demand from technology and information is having on our minds and bodies. There has been a huge increase in anxiety and depression in the modern world, especially among teenagers as they grapple with a new era of social media. Marco Grados, an associate professor at Johns Hopkins Hospital, comments on the effect social media is having on young people: 'It's all about the self-image: who's "liking" them, who's watching them, who clicked on their picture. Everything can turn into something negative. Kids are exposed to that day after day, and it's not good for them.'[20]

Meditation works on a number of levels but, first and foremost, it's incredibly effective at shifting the body out of a sympathetic nervous system state, otherwise known as the fight or flight response in the body, and into the calming, healing parasympathetic nervous system, also known as the rest and digest state. When the body goes through this shift, incredible changes take place. Instead of pumping cortisol and adrenaline into the blood, the body starts releasing: melatonin (to help us sleep), serotonin (which makes us feel happy) and oxytocin (which induces feelings of love). Our brain functionality improves as we experience a whole-brain coherence, and our body starts restoring balance through the deep rest that results from a still mind. The benefits of meditation are vast, ranging from reducing anxiety, cholesterol levels, blood pressure and adrenal fatigue, to healing depression, improving sleep and slowing the effects of ageing, among many, many other benefits.

Many people struggle to find the time to meditate because they feel they could be 'doing so much more' than sitting in stillness with their eyes closed. Everything we do is inspired by the quest to be fulfilled; it drives every action, whether it's cleaning the bathroom floor, going to a rock concert, sleeping or meditating in a monastery in Tibet—it's all a search to find fulfilment. So, with that in mind, the question is, are you fulfilled? Are you living healthily, happily, full of lightness and joy?

The price we pay for 'doing more' and 'getting more' is that we get stressed, anxious, tired and unwell. Seeking fulfilment from the outer world will give us small doses at times, but it also leaves us disappointed and wanting more. No doubt you've heard the saying 'Do less, achieve more'; well this also applies to meditation. By sitting in stillness, we rest our mind and body, and begin to restore balance. I recommend you do your own research and find out for yourself by trying it. What is life like if you meditate once in the morning and once in the afternoon? What is life like if you meditate once a day? What is life like if you don't meditate at all? This is a great experiment and one I highly recommend. Try this for a few weeks and assess the results.

When I learned to meditate and the teacher suggested two sessions a day for 20 minutes, I nearly fell off the chair—there was no way I would be able to fit that in. But I set about finding a way to make it work. I realised my day consisted of 72 segments of 20 minutes, and each one of those had been allocated to me for seeking fulfilment. Yet I was miserable, anxious and stressed. So I decided to set aside two blocks of 20 minutes, which still left 70 to do all the things I wanted to do in my day. It was ample time. So if you're struggling to fit meditation into your day, just break it down like this. And if it's going to be a 10 minute meditation, then you still have 143 segments of 10 minutes left in your day to find fulfilment in other areas.

To help you incorporate meditation into your day, I've mapped out some steps. First, some tips on how to prepare for your meditation, then some simple meditation techniques that will help you get started.

PREPARING FOR YOUR MEDITATION PRACTICE

Sit comfortably in a chair. If you're extremely flexible and it suits you, you can try sitting in a cross-legged or lotus position, but this isn't essential at all. I recommend being as comfortable as possible in your meditation, and so a padded lounge chair with a back on it is a great place to start.

Allow 10–20 minutes for your meditation practice. Of course, you can do it for five minutes or even one minute, but to start noticing more of the effects, 10–20 minutes is ideal.

Find a place where you won't be disturbed and there's as little stimulus for your senses as possible. If there's wind, hot sun, background noise, flies or other insects, you'll find that your attention is drawn to the senses, which are processing that information of the outer world, and this will pull you out of your meditation. Remember, we're going inwards here and the senses move outward, so a space that has as few stimuli as possible will be better for your senses getting started. This isn't a rule; I've meditated on train stations during peak hour and still found inner peace.

Use a timer or watch to track your time. This will allow you to surrender to your meditation so that you won't have to keep opening your eyes to check the time. However, the sound of the timer notifying you when your time is up may cut off a deep meditation if you've dived into a quiet place. It's up to you. If you have time, and don't need to restrict yourself, then you can luxuriate into a long meditation and, if you need to peek one eye open to check the time, then you can do this. Otherwise, set your timer for the desired time and surrender to your meditation.

Turn your phone to airplane mode or turn it off completely. Even if your phone is on silent, it may still cause a pulling effect on your mind as you feel drawn to engage with your phone. Our phones are designed to hold our attention, so shutting it down completely will liberate the mind from wandering in that direction.

Setting up your space can be a nice ritual. It's not essential and I don't want to promote the idea that you need paraphernalia to meditate. Ideally, we should be able to meditate anywhere and anytime, but when we have a nice space set aside for meditation and it's a space we go to regularly for stillness, the body will appreciate and recognise this process and start the meditation experience even before you're meditating. This may sound strange, but think of how you feel before you get on a roller-coaster ride. Already, your heart is beating faster and adrenaline is moving through your veins. This also happens in the opposite way when we're lighting a candle, burning incense, wrapping a shawl around our shoulders and fluffing the pillows on the chair: the body is sensing that the process of meditation is impending and it starts to de-excite before the meditation. So if you have a room set up for your meditation and a ritual to go through beforehand, this can help you prepare.

Now that we've prepared our meditation space, it's time to meditate. There are many different styles of meditation, just as there are different styles of food for different tastes. To simplify things, I've made three categories: Concentration meditation, Contemplation meditation and Transcending meditation.

CONCENTRATION MEDITATION

Concentration meditation is when we focus the mind on one still point. This may be uncomfortable and challenging, as the mind won't want to do this, but with discipline and practise, you'll be able to maintain more control over your mind.

Step 1) Close your eyes.

Step 2) Observe the simple, natural breath moving in and out of your body. It's unforced and effortless.

Step 3) As the air moves in and out of your body, observe it passing through your nostrils. As it moves through your nostrils, move your attention even closer still to the cooling skin around the rim of your nostrils.

Step 4) Keep the attention on this single point of the cooling skin around the rim of this nostril. As your mind moves away to other things, continue to bring it back. It's okay for your mind to move away from the single point; the key to this meditation is to keep bringing it back.

Step 5) Keep this focus for a minimum of 10 minutes. In time, if you wish, you can build it up to 20 minutes or longer.

As you can see, this is a very simple breath meditation. There's one thing we can rely on while we're alive, and that's for our breath to be there night and day. Buddhist monk Ajahn Amaro once quoted his master Ajah Chah saying, 'If you have time to breathe, you have time to meditate. You breathe when you walk. You breathe when you stand. You breathe when you lie down.'[19]

CONTEMPLATION MEDITATION

Contemplation meditation is a technique where we're guiding the mind to a particular place. Usually our mind is fluctuating between 50,000 –70,000 thoughts a day which are often random or negative, such as worry, regret, guilt or anger. In contemplation meditation, we're going to be very specific about the nature of thoughts. It requires being proactive with your thinking mind rather than reactive. You can use a guide to help you move your mind in a particular direction, or you can do this yourself if you feel capable of it.

In this meditation, we'll be moving our awareness to our heart space. There's a saying: 'Where the attention goes it grows.' Very rarely do we place our awareness on the heart centre and expand the feeling of inner love. Most of our lives we seek love from external sources, like other people, gifts or money. In this practice, we'll start to give our internal love centre some attention and, as a result, over time, you'll experience more love within yourself.

Step 1) Sit in a chair comfortably and close your eyes.

Step 2) Take three deep breaths, filling your lungs and exhaling.

Step 3) Return to your natural breath and place your mind's awareness into your chest cavity. Imagine a big spaciousness inside your chest.

Step 4) In the centre of your chest, imagine now a golden ball of light, like an orb, the size of a grapefruit or softball. Feel the light and warmth and lovingness from that ball in the centre of your chest. Keep your awareness on this ball of light for a few minutes, feeling it glow and radiate love and warmth in the centre of your chest.

Step 5) Now imagine the radiance and warmth of this orb of light spreading down into your belly, filling up the entire space in your stomach and lower back.

Step 6) Observe now how this light of love and warmth spreads down through the hollowness of your right leg and then down through the hollowness of your left leg, until it fills both legs all the way to the tips of your toes.

Step 7) Bring your awareness back up to the orb in your chest spreading light and love up through your chest, into your shoulders and down through your right arm, then down through your left arm, filling both arms all the way to the tips of your fingers with radiant love and light.

Step 8) Now feel the light of the orb spreading all the way up through your neck into your head space, filling your entire head with a lightness, softness and lovingness.

Step 9) Now your whole body is filled with light and love. You feel radiant, clear, light and warm with the glow of love. This is you, letting go of everything, and simply being filled with radiant loving light.

TRANSCENDING MEDITATION

Transcending meditation is a deep meditation that takes your mind beyond your thoughts. In this spaciousness, you'll experience a stillness, quietness and presence that is the absence of thought.

This type of meditation uses mantras, which is a Sanskrit word that means 'mind vehicle'. A mantra is something that guides or charms the mind into deeper states of awareness. Imagine the mind like the ocean. On the surface, there are lots of waves and, as you go deeper, there's less activity. This is like the mind. On the surface, there are thoughts, then as you go deeper into the field of the mind, there'll be less mental activity. The mind doesn't usually move in that direction, because it finds thinking on the surface very alluring. This is where the mantras come into play. They have the effect of charming the mind into deeper states.

This is a powerful meditation, because when the mind goes into these states, the body goes into a profoundly deep state of rest that can start throwing off stresses. For this reason, I recommend finding qualified teachers in your area to guide you through this process and support you with your meditation practice. You can find many transcending meditation teachers by searching in your local area for transcendental meditation, Vedic meditation, primordial sound technique or the Art of Living centres.

These meditation techniques can start you on your journey through the portal into stillness. It's in stillness that we can move beyond our stories, our past, our future and discover the essence of who we are … in our simplest form. To find out more about meditation and transformation, visit www.entertheportal.com.

'When people trust that

their bodies can heal themselves,

that their bodies can teach,

and they can enter stillness,

stillness is a wondrous state,

and it touches a truth.'

RABBI RONNIE CAHANA

RESOURCES

If you'd like to learn more about meditation, stillness and the other ideas discussed in this book, we recommend exploring the following resources. Note that a live version of this page is also available at www.entertheportal.com.

Books

Abundance: The Future Is Better Than You Think,
   by Peter H. Diamandis and Steven Kotler

Becoming Supernatural, by Dr Joe Dispenza

Bhagavad Gita, translated by Maharishi Mahesh Yogi

Calm Clarity: How to Use Science to Rewire Your Brain for Greater Wisdom, Fulfillment, and Joy, compiled by Due Quach

Emmanuel's Book: A Manual for Living Comfortably in the Cosmos,
   by Pat Rodegast and Judith Stanton

Finite and Infinite Games by James P. Corse

Into the Magic Shop: A Neurosurgeon's Quest to Discover the Mysteries of the Brain and the Secrets of the Heart, by Dr James R. Doty

Oneness, by Rasha

The Point of Existence: Transformations of Narcissism in Self-realization,
   by A.H. Almaas

The Power of Now: A Guide to Spiritual Enlightenment,
   by Eckhart Tolle

Sapiens: A Brief History of Humankind, by Yuval Noah Harari

The Science of Being and Art of Living, by Maharishi Mahesh Yogi

*Stealing Fire: How Silicon Valley, the Navy SEALs, and Maverick
    Scientists Are Revolutionizing the Way We Live and Work*,
    by Steven Kotler and Jamie Wheal

*The Wisdom of Not Knowing: Discovering a Life of Wonder by
    Embracing Uncertainty*, by Estelle Frankel

The Yoga Vasistha, by Swami Venkatesananda

Films

Baraka

I Heart Huckabees

Knight of Cups

Samsara

The Matrix

Tree of Life

What the Bleep Do We Know?

Podcasts

Collective Insights, hosted by Daniel Schmachtenberger
(neurohacker.com/collective_insights_podcast)

Future Thinkers, hosted by Euvie Ivanova and Mike Gilliland
(futurethinkers.org)

The Tim Ferriss Show, hosted by Tim Ferriss (tim.blog/podcast)

Making Sense, hosted by Sam Harris (samharris.org/podcast)

Courses

www.entertheportal.com

Websites

Amandine Roche
amandineroche.com
www.inner-peacecorps.org

Daniel Schmachtenberger
civilizationemerging.com

Dr Julia Mossbridge
www.mossbridgeinstitute.com

Due Quach
www.calmclarity.org
www.collectivesuccess.org

Heather Hennessy
heatherhennessy.com

Jacqui Fifer
www.jacquififer.com

James R. Doty MD
www.ccare.stanford.edu
www.jamesrdotymd.com
www.intothemagicshop.com

Kitra Cahana
kitracahana.com/home

Mikey Siegel
cohack.life
mikeysiegel.com

Ron 'Booda' Taylor
www.boodabear.com
www.theiinspireproject.com

Ronnie Cahana
rabbicahana.wordpress.com

The Portal
www.entertheportal.com

Tom Cronin
www.tomcronin.com
www.stillnessproject.com

ABOUT THE CONTRIBUTORS

Ronnie Cahana, Rabbi (Québec, Canada)

'I'm on the front row, watching this personal revival. It's a brilliant time.'

Rabbi Ronnie Cahana has been the spiritual leader of Congregation Beth-El (Montreal), since 2001. Born in Sweden (his parents Rabbi Moshe Cahana and Hungarian Holocaust survivor and artist Alice Lok Cahana ministered to the Holocaust survivors there), the family moved to Houston, Texas, when he was a child, where they were active in the Civil Rights Movement. Rabbi Cahana has remained a committed civil rights and community activist, his vocation taking him and his family to pulpits in the US, Latin America, Sweden and Canada. He has also been committed to ecumenical causes, engaging in Christian, Moslem and Jewish dialogue.

As a spiritual man, husband and father, Rabbi Ronnie Cahana likens stillness to an enforced slowing of the passage of time that allows for a deeper enjoyment of the present. As he describes it, he feels like a Chagall man floating above the night-time rooftops, using the hours of stillness and meditation to explore the realm beyond the physical. It is in stillness that Ronnie can fully appreciate the ability of love to transcend the tangible world and, through the art of his photographer daughter Kitra, his story has become an open invitation for people to question their preconceptions of that concept. He delights in his curiosity about new beginnings and his message is that 'anything is a miracle if you want it to be'.

Kitra Cahana, documentary photographer and photo and video artist (Québec, Canada)

'It was a special time, where ... I entered into slow time: still time.'

Kitra Cahana is a recognised photographer, filmmaker and TED speaker. She is a contributing photographer to *National Geographic* magazine, and her stunning work captures the movement and richness of the human experience. She has a BA in philosophy from McGill University and an MA in visual and media anthropology from the Freie Universität in Berlin.

In the years since her father's stroke, Kitra, the eldest child of Rabbi Ronnie Cahana, has used photography as a medium to capture their time together in a project she calls *Still Man*. She says, 'How do I explain, in a photograph, the power that another human being has to either add or detract from the healing of another person? I started a process of trying to tell a story in images.' The result is an ongoing series of beautiful and mesmerising photos that blend the slowness of time, the aliveness of Ronnie's inner world and the lightness of his being.

Kitra is the recipient of numerous grants and awards, including two Canada Council Grants for the Visual Arts, a 2016 TED Senior Fellowship, a 2015 Pulitzer Center for Investigative Reporting grant, a 2014–2015 artist residency at Prim Centre, the 2013 International Center of Photography's Infinity Award, first prize for the 2010 World Press Photo, a scholarship at FABRICA in Italy and the Thomas Morgan internship at the New York Times.

James R. Doty MD, neurosurgeon, neuroscientist and founder/director of CCARE (California, USA)

'Our default mode—if you take away the distractions of modern society—is to care for another. That's just how we evolved as a species, and it's extraordinary.'

A professor of neurosurgery at Stanford University, Dr James Doty is an entrepreneur, inventor and philanthropist. He has been at the cutting edge of medical-technology development in a number of areas, including non-invasive cancer treatment using a novel radiation device. Central to his work is his research demonstrating that a compassionate lifestyle has a profound positive effect on one's mental and physical health, while also improving the lives of those around us.

James is the author of the *New York Times* bestseller *Into the Magic Shop: A Neurosurgeon's Quest to Discover the Mysteries of the Brain and Secrets of the Heart* (Hodder & Stoughton, 2016), which has since been translated into 36 languages. He is also the senior editor of *The Oxford Handbook of Compassion Science* (Oxford University Press, 2017).

Heather Hennessy, former US national track athlete and national Fox Sports presenter (California, USA)

'What's better than teaching kids about mindfulness and how to start on their own spiritual path?'

Heather Hennessy's life has been a lesson in reinvention, with meditation playing a key part in connecting to her deeper, more intuitive self. For Heather, it was the journey from forced stillness to intentional stillness that provided a pathway to strengthening her inner voice and ceasing the cycles of people-pleasing and fear that had led her to pursue physical strength over inner strength during her youth. Healing childhood wounds and understanding and forgiving her father for generational patterns they have both experienced has enabled the two to break that cycle and enjoy a fresh start in their relationship free from years-old anger or resentment. It's led to both father and daughter experiencing more joy in their lives now, and has paved the way to a new career for Heather helping others move through 'the rollercoaster of life'.

Heather now works to inspire women and children to find their power by listening to their intuition, so they can live a life that is authentic to who they are on the inside. Heather continues to work on a series of books and TV episodes for children designed to help kids engage with mindfulness from a young age. She is also involved in an interview series on healing with 10 special guests who have helped or inspired Heather on her own journey.

Dr Julia Mossbridge, cognitive neuroscientist, futurist and Loving AI principal investigator (California, USA)

'We may only need one generation before we transform the world.'

Dr Julia Mossbridge is a futurist trained in cognitive neuroscience whose focus is on teaching and learning about love and time. In addition to being the founder and research director of Mossbridge Institute, LLC, Dr Mossbridge is a visiting scholar in the Psychology Department at Northwestern University, a fellow at the Institute of Noetic Sciences, Science Director at Focus@Will Labs, and an associated professor in Integral and Transpersonal Psychology at the California Institute of Integral Studies.

Dr Mossbridge is currently engaged in three love-centred projects: the Loving AI project; a project examining whether hypnosis can be used to induce a state of unconditional love; and consciously bringing unconditional love into the lives of the tech workers and executives she coaches. She is also principal investigator on multiple projects related to recognition and the possibility of time travel. She also invented and patented Choice Compass, a physiologically based decision-making app.

Dr Mossbridge is the author of *The Calling: A 12-Week Science-Based Program to Discover, Energize, and Engage Your Soul's Work*; (New Harbinger, 2019) and *The Garden: An Inside Experiment*. She is also the co-author, with Imants Barus, of *Transcendent Mind: Re-thinking the Science of Consciousness* (APA Books, 2017), and with Theresa Cheung, of *The Premonition Code: The Science of Precognition* (Watkins Media, 2018).

Due Quach, social entrepreneur and founder of Calm Clarity (Pennsylvania, USA)

'When you get the opportunity to make the world a better place, you just can't walk away from it.'

A refugee from Vietnam who grew up in inner-city Philadelphia, Due Quach (pronounced 'Zway Kwok') beat the odds to graduate from Harvard College and the Wharton School of Business and then build an international career in management consulting and private equity investments. After struggling to find satisfaction with conventional success, she embarked on a personal quest to heal trauma and understand 'real happiness' by integrating Western neuroscience with Eastern traditions.

Due developed Calm Clarity, a neuroscience-based approach to developing mindful leadership and addressing unconscious bias, which shares mind hacking tools that enable people and organisations to break limiting patterns, realise their full potential and make a positive impact on the world. She also creates social impact through the Collective Success Network, a non-profit she founded that partners with companies to support and mentor low-income first-generation college students, and advocate for socioeconomic inclusiveness and diversity in higher education and professional workplaces.

Due is the founder and CEO of the social enterprise Calm Clarity and author of *Calm Clarity: How to Use Science to Rewire Your Brain for Greater Wisdom, Fulfillment and Joy* (Penguin Random House, 2018), which was one of Fast Company's seven best books of 2018.

Amandine Roche, human rights expert and founder of Amanuddin Foundation (Paris, France)

'I've been working on the peace process, democratisation and human rights for 15 years, and peace is not in the head. Peace is in the heart.'

For 15 years, human rights expert Amandine Roche committed her life to building global peace through democratisation, women's empowerment and civic education. In the course of her work for the UN, she was exposed to extreme environments and the daily threat of attack, kidnap and murder.

Meditation and yoga gave Amandine tools to cope with the atrocities she had witnessed and regain her tranquillity. She now teaches these same tools to humanitarian workers and refugees living and working in similar circumstances, aiming to help them achieve inner peace as the foundation for global peace-building.

In 2011, Amandine founded the Amanuddin Foundation in Kabul, Afghanistan, and subsequently launched the Inner Peace Corps to implement a program for international peacekeepers. She is the author of several French-language books, including *Le Vol des Colombes* (Robert Laffont, 2005), a diary of her experiences in Afghanistan.

Daniel Schmachtenberger, evolutionary philosopher and global systems strategist (California, USA)

'We live at the most critical, meaningful inflexion point possible.'

As a thought-leader and advocate for social change, Daniel Schmachtenberger's work centres on civilisation design, developing economic and governmental systems that incentivise life-enhancing behaviour, decentralise problem solving, and foster conscious participation. Growing up home-schooled, Daniel had early exposure to design science (Buckminster Fuller, Jacques Fresco, Permaculture, etc.), systems science and complexity (Fritjof Capra, Stuart Kauffman, etc.), philosophy and psychology (Eastern and Western approaches), and activism (animal rights, environmental issues, social justice, etc.) His passion has always been at the intersection of these topics—specifically, facilitating the emergence into a mature civilisation—that can prevent otherwise-impending catastrophes, remediate existing damage, make possible a radically higher quality of life for all sustainably, and support greater realisation of our individual and collective potential.

He is the co-founder and director of Research and Development at Neurohacker Collective, working on complexity informed solutions for the future of wellbeing science, medicine and evolving human capacity. He hosts a podcast there exploring those topics.

Mikey Siegel, robotics engineer and transformative technology developer (California, USA)

'This is about our greatest potential as a human species.'

Mikey Siegel is working on a life in flow, asking questions like: Can technology be a tool to help us realise a profound sense of peace and wellbeing? Can the devices around us do more than provide information and change behaviour? What if our gadgets guided us towards a deep sense of connection with ourselves and each other?

Mikey started his journey as an engineer, working in the area of Human Robot Interaction at the MIT Media Lab. He has since become a pioneer in his field, working at the intersection of technology and wellbeing. His goal is to understand and enhance human happiness from an engineering perspective.

A lecturer at Stanford University, Mikey believes that we can change the world from the inside out. He seeks to explore the ways technology can help humankind towards a more mindful and peaceful existence. Mikey is the founder of the consciousness hacking movement and the co-founder of the Transformative Technology Conference.

Ron 'Booda' Taylor, retired US Army sergeant
(Georgia, USA)

*'Life throws challenges at us all the time. There's always adversity.
So we can step up and rise to the occasion, or we can do nothing
and let it consume us. I'm not a "do nothing" person.'*

After a 25-year military career, Ron 'Booda' Taylor received medical retirement due to traumatic brain injury and post-traumatic stress disorder (PTSD). Booda's efforts to make stillness an everyday part of his life are proving an effective tool in managing his PTSD symptoms and his reintegration into civilian society.

Booda had considered forging a post-military career out of his passion for cooking, but a change in mindset from culinary arts to helping and inspiring people drove him to create the INSPIRE Project. His desire to give back to the type of community he came from led him to start contacting schools throughout the United States about the opportunity to speak with students. His first engagement was for a high school junior ROTC (reserve officer training program) where he shared how joining the military had helped this self-described 'knucklehead' grow up and realise that he wasn't 'a lost soul'. Tracking from how he started out to how the military helped him get his life together—and taught him he 'was salvageable'—he told the kids it was a good avenue to get a foothold on life. The ROTC instructor was so impressed that she introduced him to the counsellor, who invited him to speak to the graduating classes. And it's snowballed from there.

Whether he's addressing groups of graduating students from similar types of backgrounds to his about life after high school or issues they face on a daily basis—asking: 'How many times have you been told you'll "never amount to anything", or that you'll end up "dead or in jail", or "pregnant before you're 15" et cetera?—or whether he's talking to kids at a shelter as young as six about coming from a broken home, Booda's skill comes from connecting with children where they're at. He uses his own story and a straightforward, honest approach to let young people know that it's possible to respond to their environment in a different way and that none of that should stop anyone from achieving their dream. His message: Don't let anyone or anything decide your future for you.

'Every moment is the

start of a new life.

It's a brand new awakening.'

RABBI RONNIE CAHANA

THANKS

Spiritual leader Ram Dass once said, 'If you think you're enlightened, go spend a week with your family.' As creators of *The Portal*, we feel a more appropriate saying would be: 'If you think you're enlightened, go and make a film and write a book.'

This project has been six years in the making. It has tested and challenged us more times than we care to recall, and it would not have been possible without the support of many phenomenal people.

We set out to find stories of remarkable transformation involving stillness that would awe, inspire and represent the potential for change that exists within each of us. A small, passionate team of journalists and filmmakers conducted a worldwide search for human stories over many months. Sarah Hudson, Georgia Darlow, Michelle Thomas, Ann Buchner, Adam Farrow-Palmer and Flavia Abdurahman worked with us meticulously during this process, reading scientific papers, digging up newspaper articles, trawling the web and social media, and reaching out to myriad teachers, schools, scientists, meditation instructors, experts, entrepreneurs—even astronauts—to find the most powerful narratives for this book. Special thanks to the inimitable Georgia Darlow and Sarah Hudson who led our research team. Your relentless passion for the project, sharp noses for the perfect story, humour and persistence amid all manner of tall and near-impossible requests, and the lateral approaches you applied in our worldwide search for all things transformative and 'still', led us to the powerful and thought-provoking interviews included in this collection.

Paul Currie and Naomi Jensen, you were the gentle guiding force to keep us focused and on track. Your creative insights and deep passion for human stories have left an indelible mark on this work.

Gary Woodyard and Mat Graham, thank you for your openness to exploring new ideas with us, for being sounding boards and confidants, day and night, for your unflagging commitment, support and zeal. They have been invaluable.

To Richard Van Every and Heather Hollander, from the moment we met in San Diego at that party we knew there was a great connection. You two were the supporting foundation for this project. Your deep passion for the film played a big part in shaping what is today, *The Portal*. Thank you for your creative guidance and for living with such open hearts.

To Ellenor Cox, thank you for postponing your retirement from film in order to grace us with your expertise in film and with your deep understanding of spirituality and mindset. You were a solid sounding board and mentor that some upstart first-time producers needed very much.

To Nick Broadhurst, together we gave birth to this idea many years ago: 'Let's make a movie to inspire the world to meditate.' We planted a seed and it grew, blossomed and bloomed to become a global movement. Thank you for the inspiration and getting the ball rolling.

David Whealy and the team at DWA, thank you for the gazillion contracts that you pulled together and for your sage legal advice. You were our steady guide through the incredibly complex world of filmmaking and finance.

To Kelly Doust, Julie Mazur Tribe, Andrea O'Connor, Vivien Valk, Madeleine Kane, Lou Johnson, Lou Playfair, Carol Warwick and the rest of the awesome team at Murdoch Books, thank you for believing in us and guiding us to shape this book. Your grounded views and deft touch have been such an asset throughout this process. We are so grateful you share our intention to make the planet a better place to live.

To Josh Pomeranz, Adam Scott, Cat Armstrong and the entire team at Spectrum Films, you were there from the very beginning, offering us the support we needed to make this all happen. It took us some time to get there, but, patiently and consistently, there you were. Thank you!

To our financial supporters, Michael Taylor, Darren Perry, Will Britten, David Ioannidis, Colin and Tamara Gilbert, Solomon Steadman, Dmitriy Bataev, Shashi and Priya Vaswani, John McKenzie, Carol Look and VentureCrowd, a HUGE thank you ... none of this could have happened without your support for this project.

Hundreds of people from diverse backgrounds generously shared their deep and sometimes devastating personal stories during an interview process that was intense and incredibly moving. To all the extraordinary individuals who shared their personal stories or life's work, brainstormed ideas or suggested important connections, this book would not have been possible without your generosity and honesty. And to Booda, Due, Heather, Jim, Amandine, Mikey, Julia, Daniel, Kitra and the beam of shining light that is Ronnie, we are so deeply grateful to create this with you, and bring your stories and message to the world.

Finally, to all the sages, saints, lightworkers and healers who have paved the way to making this project possible, your wisdom and commitment to elevating life on earth are what have inspired us to carry on with your work. Thank you for your eternal light.

From Tom

A deep, deep gratitude to my family—Jen, Taj and Lauren—who have listened to the drama unfold every day for many years. You have surrendered your father and husband countless times to being on the road filming, in production meetings, or countless Voxers, Skype and phone calls. You have been a source of grounding, feedback and encouragement through thick and thin. You're my inspiration. I have an unbounded amount of gratitude and love for you all!

To Mum and Dad, I know you thought I was crazy many times for taking on this project, but there you were, always there for me. Thank you for your endless love and guidance.

To Jacqui, your tireless determination, commitment and vision for this project is immeasurable. This couldn't have happened without you—this did happen because of you. Thank you for your passion for excellence, for pushing me to continually reach higher, further, deeper than I thought possible. Words are too finite for the gratitude I have for you.

From Jacqui

To Ramon, Kyla, Gary, Mat, Georgie, Naomi, Elle, Heather, Booda, Bruce, Radek, Vicente, Maria and many more treasured friends who have cheered me on from the sidelines: your collective spirit imbues these pages, and the last few years would not have been anywhere near as rich or meaningful without you. Thank you for waiting patiently and welcomingly with open arms and hearts, for finding ways to make me laugh when I wanted to cry, for urging me to go further and deeper than I ever thought possible, for continually shifting and expanding my perspective with your own unique brand of wisdom, for tirelessly listening to different versions of the same themes over and over again, and for understanding when I had too much to say to say anything at all.

To my family, who have each supported me in their own personal way, thank you for always embracing my unconventional path and for instilling in me the beauty of both the mystical and practical aspects of life.

To my Spanish family, your unconditional love opened a doorway in my heart.

To François, Dan, Pinky and the rest of the crew—whose support, commitment, agility and humour have always been a source of inspiration—your artistry and gentle ways helped give this baby form.

And to Tom, thank you for believing that I was the right person to accompany you on your long journey to bring a dream alive.

NOTES

Introduction

1. Noam Chomsky, 'a perfect storm', see 'Noam Chomsky in Conversation with Amy Goodman on Climate Change, Nukes, Syria, WikiLeaks & More', *Democracy Now*, 29 May 2017, www.democracynow.org/2017/5/29/ noam_chomsky_in_conversation_with_amy.

One: The programming begins

2. 'Since wars begin in the minds of men, it is in the minds of men that the defences of peace must be constructed', see UNESCO Constitution from the United Nations (signed 16 November 1945), portal.unesco.org/en/ ev.php-URL_ID=15244&URL_DO=DO_TOPIC&URL_SECTION=201.html.

Two: Conditioned into a win-lose system

3. Due Quach, 'College is a time of self-discovery, but it is particularly hard to find who you are when you attend one of the most intensely competitive, hyper-critical and hypocritical universities on the planet', see 'Poor and Traumatized at Harvard', 4 January 2016, Medium, medium.com/@ duequach/poor-and-traumatized-at-harvard-e5938b702207.

4. Robin Dunbar, 'Dunbar Number', *How Many Friends Does One Person Need?: Dunbar's Number and Other Evolutionary Quirks*, Harvard University Press, Cambridge, Massachusetts, 2010.

5. The Philadelphia Urban ACE Study (2013), funded by the Robert Wood Johnson Foundation and conducted by Public Health Management Corporation (PHMC) for the Institute for Safe Families and the ACE Task Force, www.instituteforsafefamilies.org/philadelphia-urban-ace-study.

Three: Brink of a phase shift

6.   Tim Ferriss, 'Most people will choose unhappiness over uncertainty', *The 4-Hour Work Week: Escape the 9–5, Live Anywhere and Join the New Rich*, Crown Archetype, New York, 2010.

7.   Charles Darwin, 'It's not the strongest of the species that survives, but the most adaptable', attributed to Darwin, but first paraphrased in a speech delivered in 1963 by a Louisiana State University business professor named Leon C. Megginson at the convention of the Southwestern Social Science Association. The text of his address was published in the quarterly journal of the association. Megginson presented his own idiosyncratic interpretation of the central idea outlined in Darwin's *On the Origin of Species*. Megginson did not use quotation marks: 'it is not the most intellectual of the species that survives; it is not the strongest that survives; but the species that survives is the one that is able best to adapt and adjust to the changing environment in which it finds itself.' It has since been adopted and paraphrased by many writers and academics to communicate Darwin's idea. See also Charles Darwin, 'As many more individuals of each species are born than can possibly survive; and as, consequently, there is a frequently recurring struggle for existence, it follows that any being, if it vary however slightly in any manner profitable to itself, under the complex and sometimes varying conditions of life, will have a better chance of surviving, and thus be naturally selected. From the strong principle of inheritance, any selected variety will tend to propagate its new and modified form', *On the Origin of Species*, 1859.

8.   The Organisation for Economic Co-operation and Development (OECD), global statistics. Australia has one of the highest rates of obesity and one of the highest uses of antidepressants per capita, see www.oecd.org/australia/Health-at-a-Glance-2015-Key-Findings-AUSTRALIA.pdf; Sky Gould and Lauren F. Friedman, 'Antidepressant Use is Rising Sharply around the World', Business Insider, 7 October 2016, www.businessinsider.com.au/countries-largest-antidepressant-drug-users-2016-11?r=US&IR=T.

9.   Dr Vernon Barnes et al., 'Impact of Transcendental Meditation on Psychotropic Medication Use among Active Duty Military Service Members with Anxiety and PTSD', *Military Medicine*, vol. 181, no. 1, 2016, pp. 56–63, www.academia.edu/36219957/

Impact_of_Transcendental_Meditation_on_Psychotropic_Medication_Use_
Among_Active_Duty_Military_Service_Members_With_Anxiety_and_PTSD;
Christopher Bergland, 'Meditation Reduces Post-Traumatic Stress
Disorder Symptoms', *Psychology Today*, 13 January 2016, www.
psychologytoday.com/au/blog/the-athletes-way/201601/
meditation-reduces-post-traumatic-stress-disorder-symptoms.

10. Isaac Asimov, *I, Robot, Robot and Foundation* series, see www.asimovonline.
com/asimov_home_page.html; and www.britannica.com/biography/
Isaac-Asimov.

11. Oscar G. Anderson, American Association of Retired Persons (AARP),
estimates that we're somewhere between two and three times lonelier now
than we were 50 years ago, 'Loneliness Among Older Adults: A National
Survey of Adults 45+', AARP Research, September 2010, www.aarp.org/
research/topics/life/info-2014/loneliness_2010.html; www.aarp.org/content/
dam/aarp/research/surveys_statistics/life-leisure/2018/loneliness-social-
connections-2018.doi.10.26419-2Fres.00246.001.pdf; and www.aarp.org/
content/dam/aarp/research/surveys_statistics/general/2012/loneliness-2010.
doi.10.26419%252Fres.00064.001.pdf.

12. The Harvard Study of Adult Development, www.adultdevelopmentstudy.org.

13. Dan Ariely, research showing human beings are fundamentally driven by
impact, in *The Upside of Irrationality: The Unexpected Benefits of Defying
Logic*, Harper Perennial, New York, 2011.

Four: Through the portal of stillness

14. Reference documentaries on waste, minimalism and the excess of modern
society: multiple authors, directed by Cosima Dannoritzer and Steve
Michelson, *The Lightbulb Conspiracy* (*AKA Pyramids of Waste*): *The Untold
Story of Planned Obsolescence*, 2010; and directed by Martin Borgs, *Overdose:
The Next Financial Crisis*, 2010.

15. Ray Dalio, 'meditation has probably been the single most important reason
for whatever success I've had', Twitter post, 14 February 2018, twitter.com/
raydalio/status/963797553098711041?lang=en.

16. Statistics taken from 'Number of Mobile Phone Users Worldwide from 2015
to 2020 (in Billions)', Statista, 2019, www.statista.com/statistics/274774/
forecastof-mobile-phone-users-worldwide; Mobile Fact Sheet', Pew Research

Center, 5 February 2018, www.pewinternet.org/fact-sheet/mobile; Rani Molla, 'Two-thirds of Adults Worldwide Will Own Smartphones Next Year', Recode, 16 October 2017, www.recode.net/2017/10/16/16482168/two-thirds-ofadults-worldwide-will-own-smartphones-next-year; Paul Sawers, '5 Billion People Now Have a Mobile Phone Connection, According to GSMA Data', Venture Beat, 13 June 2017, venturebeat.com/2017/06/13/5-billion-people-now-have-a-mobile-phone-connection-according-to-gsma-data.

17. Richard Rohr, 'Pain that is not transformed is transmitted', see *On the Threshold of Transformation: Daily Meditations for Men*, Loyola Press, Chicago, 2010.

18. In 1957, UN Secretary General Dag Hammarskjöld reopened the meditation room at the United Nations headquarters with this speech: 'A Room of Quiet', UN, www.un.org/depts/dhl/dag/meditationroom.htm.

An introduction to meditation

19. See the Chopra Center for more daily inspiration: chopra.com/daily-inspiration.

20. Amy Ellis Nutt citing Marco Grados, 'Why Kids and Teens Face Far More Anxiety These Days', *Washington Post*, 15 May 2018, www.washingtonpost.com/news/to-your-health/wp/2018/05/10/why-kids-and-teens-may-face-far-more-anxiety-these-days/?utm_term=.416fe4767a6b.

21. Ajahn Chah, cited by Ajahn Amaro, in Barbara Gates and Wes Nisker (eds), *The Best of Inquiring Mind: 25 Years of Dharma, Drama, and Uncommon Insight*, Wisdom Publications, Somerville Massachusetts, 2008, p. 21.

ABOUT THE
AUTHORS

Tom Cronin

Tom Cronin spent 26 years in finance markets as one of Sydney's leading bond and swap brokers. He discovered meditation in the early stages of his career, when the anxiety and chaos he was experiencing had hit a crisis point, and it completely transformed his world, both personally and professionally. Tom went on to study meditation and Eastern philosophy in India, Bali and Australia, ultimately gaining his teaching qualification.

Tom is passionate about reducing stress and chaos in people's lives. In recognition of the potential this ancient practice has for personal healing and human development, he founded the Stillness Project, a global movement to inspire one billion people to sit in stillness daily. Tom's ongoing work in transformational leadership and cultivating inner peace through meditation takes him around the world, hosting retreats, mentoring, presenting keynote talks, teaching and creating *The Portal* film—book experience—all part of his commitment to the current planetary shift.

Tom is the author of six books for adults: *Insights*; *The Path to Peace: A Guide to Living with Ease in a Rapidly Changing World*; *Spirit and Soul: Exploring the Seven States of Consciousness*; *Faster Deeper Sleep: The Ultimate Guide to a Daily Recharge*; and *Faster Deeper Calm: How to Live Without Anxiety and Panic*. He is also the author of a children's book, *Missy Moo Meditates*.

Jacqui Fifer

Jacqui Fifer is a passionate filmmaker with a commitment to authentic storytelling and a taste for big visions. Jacqui has led teams from development through to post and visual effects on several feature films. She was producer of the multi-award-winning dramatic feature *Concealed* (2017) and a key player in such films as *Better Watch Out* (2016), *The Osiris Child* (2016) and *Infini* (2015). While based in Spain, she co-directed the 2012 and 2013 Dones en Art (Women and Film) festivals.

For Jacqui, life is work is joy is life—there is no separation—and the former Ibiza DJ brings a philosophy of seamlessness and union to everything she does. What emerges is a unique marrying of sound, words, images and heart that moves the soul. An advocate of human capacity development, she is thrilled to turn her hand to a subject close to her heart. *The Portal* is her first feature documentary.

PHOTO © DAN FREENE ACS